BASEBALL STARS OF TOMORROW
An Inside Look at the Minor Leagues

by BILL GUTMAN

ACE TEMPO BOOKS, NEW YORK

BASEBALL STARS OF TOMORROW
Copyright © 1982 by Bill Gutman
All rights reserved. No part of this book may be reproduced in any form or by any means, except for the inclusion of brief quotations in a review, without permission in writing from the publisher.

An Ace Tempo Original

ISBN: 0-448-16937-1

This Printing: August 1982

Tempo Books is registered in the United States Patent Office

Published simultaneously in Canada

Manufactured in the United States of America

CONTENTS

Introduction	1
Prologue	7
The Organization	13
The Scouts	29
The Stars of Tomorrow	43
Dave Stewart	45
Ted Power	59
Jack Perconte	73
Ricky Wright	85
Don Crow	95
Ed Amelung	109
Brian Williams	119
Dave Anderson	127
The Managers	139
Life in the Minor Leagues	157

BASEBALL STARS OF TOMORROW
An Inside Look at the Minor Leagues

INTRODUCTION

All of the young baseball stars introduced in this book began playing the game early. They were perhaps five, six, or seven years old when they started throwing a ball around the backyard, tagging after older brothers to the local Little League field, or maybe waiting for their fathers to come home from work for a five or ten minute game of catch. I'm sure many of you who read this book have done the same thing.

I, too, was a baseball addict as a youngster and anxiously awaited that next game of catch with my father, or a chance to play two-a-cat on our narrow street, or a full-fledged softball game at elementary school. Then there were the countless imaginary games, when you pretended you were your favorite major leaguer. Ah, memories.

By the time I was nine or ten I was a veritable walking encyclopedia of baseball. In fact, I honestly think I knew more facts and figures about the history of the game and its legendary players in those days than I do now. I was ready to answer any and all questions about Ty Cobb, Christy Mathewson, the Babe, Hornsby, Wagner, Walter Johnson. In addition, I could relate baseball's poignant moments and high drama with youthful enthusiasm and emotion, events ranging from Lou Gehrig's farewell speech, to Grover Alexander fanning Tony Lazzeri in in the 1926 World Series, to Carl Hubbell striking out five straight American League superstars in the 1934 All-Star Game. All of it.

Growing up in Connecticut during this period, the late 1940s and early 1950s, I was also developing a passionate attachment for the New York Yankees. There were three baseball teams in New York then, the Yanks, the crosstown New York Giants, and those upstarts from that other borough, the Brooklyn Dodgers. For some reason, it seems that most Yankee fans always remained neutral toward the Giants, unless the two teams met head to head. As for the Dodgers, well, it was simple. You hated them.

That's just how it was, and most of the time the Yankee fans prospered, while those who lived and died with the Dodgers had a credo all their own—wait 'til next year. For whenever the Yanks and Dodgers met, it was the Bronx Bombers who invariably came out on top. I became aware of the rivalry for the first time in 1949 when the Yanks whipped the Dodgers to win the World Series. And I remember taking great pleasure the following year when the Philadelphia Phillies Whiz Kids edged the Dodgers to win the National League pennant.

Then there was 1951 and a game that will be forever etched upon my memory. I can readily recall coming home from school to see the final inning of that final pennant playoff game between the Dodgers and Giants, the Jints Bobby Thomson coming up to face Brooklyn's Ralph Branca with two on and the Giants trailing by a pair. I turned to my mother and announced that only a homer could save the Giants, though my main object wasn't to see them win as much as it was to watch the Dodgers lose.

BASEBALL STARS OF TOMORROW

What happened next will be part of baseball's folklore forever. Thomson indeed did slam a homer, the so-called shot heard round the world. The Dodgers were beaten and I then rooted the Yankees home in six against the Giants in the World Series. The next two years the Bombers were there again, this time whipping the Dodgers head-to-head. They had beaten the "Bums" in five consecutive World Series dating back to 1941. As I said, it was a real pleasure to be young and a Yankee fan back then.

But finally there came that bleak October day in 1955. It was the Yanks and Dodgers in the Fall Classic once more, and though the Dodgers had managed to take a 3-2 lead in games, I was still confident. The Yanks had Whitey Ford and Tommy Byrne ready for the final pair and I just knew they could do it. Sure enough, Ford won to knot the Series and it was then Byrne against a Dodger youngster named Johnny Podres for all the marbles.

We had school that day, and sometime in the afternoon the vice-principal came on the P.A. system. His words still cling to my memory.

"I guess you're wondering about the World Series," he said. "Well, the Dodgers won . . ."

I didn't want to hear another word. For me, that was enough. I was crushed. We Yankee fans didn't even want to lose one to the Dodgers. The same feeling flooded back some eight years later, in 1963. I was a college student then, but when the Los Angeles Dodgers met the Mantle-Maris Yankees it was suddenly like old times. Down in Maryland, Yankee fans were in a minority, so the few of us New Yorkers were totally destroyed when Sandy Koufax, Don Drysdale, and that same Johnny Podres blew the Yankees away in four straight games.

That, in a sense was the end of an era. When the two clubs finally met again in 1977, things weren't quite the same. The players had changed and so had the old loyalties. Sure, I was still a Yankee fan, but I didn't view the Dodgers with the same kind of venom anymore. In fact, I had already written about several Dodgers players and in truth, the rivalry hadn't been quite the same since the Dodgers had moved from Brooklyn to the west coast in 1957.

Which brings us to the *Baseball Stars of Tomorrow*. When it was first proposed that I write about several minor league ballplayers, I hedged. After all, minor league players are not exactly household names and I wondered if such a book would find a readership. After several discussions it was decided to concentrate on a single minor league organization, explaining how it functions in relation to the parent club, and how the stars of the future are discovered and groomed for the major leagues.

Being that I still live in the New York area, my first instinct was to go to my old favorite team, and perhaps discover some young players who would follow in the footsteps of Ruth, Gehrig, DiMaggio, Mantle, and Reggie Jackson. However, upon making contact, it seemed that certain details for completing the project simply could not be worked out. I would now either have to scrap the whole thing or look elsewhere.

That's when I decided to contact the Dodgers. Perhaps more than any other team in baseball, the Dodgers were known for having a first class organization, well developed from top to bottom, an organization that had continually produced high caliber talent since the late 1940s. So I made a phone call, and within five minutes had an unofficial go ahead to begin the work.

BASEBALL STARS OF TOMORROW

Once the details were ironed out, the team confirmed a willingness to indeed help all it could with this project. From my first contact with Publicity Director Steve Brener and a talk with Vice President Bill Schweppe, the Director of Minor League Operations, to my eventual interviews with eight young ballplayers in the organization, I was met with nothing less than total and complete cooperation, friendliness, honesty, and a genuine eagerness to help. All this from a team I admittedly rooted against with all my sporting heart for so many years.

But, of course, looking back now at those Dodger players I thought I "hated," the old feelings have long changed. They are remembered fondly as part of my own youth and as the very great ballplayers that they were. Talking at length to the present day Dodger farmhands, I realized they could do a lot worse than following in the footsteps of Reese, Robinson, Hodges, Snider, Campanella, Furillo, Erskine, Newcombe, Koufax, Drysdale, Cey, Garvey and the rest.

So to both the Dodgers of Brooklyn and the Dodgers of Los Angeles, I take my hat off and proclaim a sincere and humble Thank You..

PROLOGUE

Minor league baseball has been around for a very long time. In fact, there were minor leagues even before the majors were formed. During baseball's infancy in the last century, any town that had an organized team which played teams from nearby towns on a regular basis and paid its players or charged admission to the games, was, in effect, a minor league team. Since there were no major leagues, these clubs were likely called simply a professional baseball club, or perhaps a semi-professional team.

But ever since the formation of first the National Baseball League and then the American Baseball League, there have been minor league teams to prepare and send players to the Bigs.

The purpose and function of the minors has changed over the years. Before big league baseball expanded to all corners of the land, the minor leagues were more widespread, often the only form of baseball for miles and miles around. Teams were independently owned by people looking to profit from a legitimate business venture. There were even times when players could earn as much or more by playing in the minor leagues than in the majors.

Today, the situation is somewhat different. Changing economic conditions and the expansion of the major leagues along with the advent of television has diminished the number of minor leagues in existence. In addition, many of the teams are now subsidized by the major league club to which they are connected. It's very difficult for an independent minor league owner to show a profit, so the major league clubs must put their money in the pot to keep the minor leagues afloat.

But afloat they will stay. Because as long as there is major league baseball, there will have to be minor leagues to provide the players with a training ground, a place to learn and get ready both physically and mentally to play in the Bigs. In that sense, the minor leagues have not changed. They have been providing the Baseball Stars of Tomorrow for a long time.

Of course, the minor leagues are also known for other things besides nurturing new talent. The long and boring bus rides are legendary, as are poor accommodations, bad food, low pay and grueling schedules with very few off days. Many of the teams are located in small, out-of-the-way towns, contributing to an atmosphere that has traditionally been anything but first rate.

But as with most other things, there have been improvements. The ballparks are for the most part better, as are the accommodations and the food. There is more travel by plane than in the past, though the long bus rides remain, especially at the lower levels. With a smaller number of teams affiliated with each major league club, there is more intensive coaching and instruction in an attempt to get the talent ready in the fastest time possible.

There are also fewer examples of the carnival atmosphere that often accompanied minor league games. Stan Wasiak, the manager of the Dodger's Class A team

BASEBALL STARS OF TOMORROW

at Vero Beach, Florida, recalls from his own playing days when a man was buried alive behind home plate and dug up after the game, all in the name of promotion. That may be a bit far-fetched, but there are still some relatively wacky promotional gimmicks today.

Nor are conditions perfect. Many of the old ballparks remain, some without locker room facilities, others with bad lighting, some just poorly constructed, like the one in Ogden, Utah, where the sun sets almost directly in centerfield, making it nearly impossible to hit the ball in the late afternoon. One of the players interviewed remembered playing a game in a park where the automatic sprinkler system was malfunctioning and kept going on without warning during the entire game. These are things which can only happen in the minor leagues.

But in spite of all this, the real product of the minors is people, youngsters who learn not only about becoming better baseball players, but also about growing and maturing, learning to function in the world whether they make the big leagues or not. For the odds are still very long. Just a few of the players who begin the trip through the minor leagues wind up in the majors. And fewer still become genuine stars. So many players have to learn how to handle disappointment, and in some cases, downright failure. It can be a hard lesson to learn.

That makes it even more important to have good people to do the teaching, and that is a mark of a real first class organization. The Dodgers, it seems, have those people from top to bottom. In *Baseball Stars of Tomorrow* you will meet some of them, beginning with Bill Schweppe, the man who runs the entire minor league operation and around whom everything else revolves. Without superb direction from the top, the rest of the organization could not be so successful.

You will also meet the man responsible for finding the

talent, Director of Scouting Ben Wade, a former major league pitcher who performed with the Dodgers when they were still in Brooklyn. Also, two fine managers, Del Crandall, a former all-star catcher with the Milwaukee Braves, and Stan Wasiak, a man who has made the minor leagues his life's work.

Crandall has managed the Dodgers top farm club, the Triple A Albuquerque Dukes, to a pair of Pacific Coast League championships. With players just a step away from the majors, Crandall seems the perfect man for the job, with his playing experience and also major league managing experience behind him.

Stan Wasiak has managed in the minors for some thirty years, and now runs the Class A Vero Beach Dodgers. His job is somewhat different from Crandall's since he is often dealing with youngsters right out of high school getting their first taste of professional ball. Both managers must work with their players on a variety of different levels.

Then there are the players themselves. As you will quickly learn, each one has a different story, different problems that had to be overcome. Some of them have been in the minors for several years, and know that they will have to make it soon, or else. They have their own special kind of pressure. Others are just starting their professional careers, and they have the pressure of living up to past performances that have often made them stars since their Little League days. These youngsters also have to cope with the pressure of being away from home and on their own, meeting new and different people for the first time, and learning about the lifestyle of a professional athlete. They must do all these while learning their trade as well and as quickly as they can.

So there is more to life in the minor leagues than just learning to run, hit, and throw. It is a multi-faceted ex-

BASEBALL STARS OF TOMORROW

perience, made even more complex by the advent of sports agents and the possibility of a huge contract somewhere down the road if a player can succeed. There are just so many different things to think about.

In the following pages, the lives and careers of eight players will unfold, along with their travels within the Los Angeles Dodgers entire organization. There is pitcher Dave Stewart, a 17th round draft choice who wasn't signed until he participated in a tryout camp. Originally a catcher, Dave made the Dodgers in 1981 as a short reliever and wound up with a World Series ring.

Ted Power is another pitcher, a hard-throwing righthander who has been in the minors since 1976. There were times in his career that Ted admits he didn't push himself hard enough, and allowed himself to feel bitterness because of his long trek. Now, after a brilliant 1981 season at Albuquerque, Power feels he is ready for the majors.

Another long term minor leaguer is second baseman Jack Perconte, who has always hit well, but been saddled with arm and fielding problems. After a solid 1981 season at Albuquerque, in which he hit .346, Perconte feels he is ready, whether it be with the Dodgers or another team. He feels if he doesn't make it now, his age will begin to work against him.

Ricky Wright is a lanky, lefthanded pitcher from Paris, Texas, who also had a fine season with the Albuquerque team in 1981, including a big exhibition victory over the parent team Dodgers right after the baseball strike ended. Ricky has had to make an adjustment of a different kind as he meets new teammates from all over the country who don't always understand his Texas lifestyle.

For Don Crow, catching was the only way to go. He says it was a matter of physical limitations. But being in that demanding spot behind the mask has put him just a whisker away from the big leagues. An anemic bat is something he has worked feverishly to improve and he's also had the foresight to complete his college education in the off-season so he can provide for his wife and growing family if baseball doesn't work out.

Ed Amelung, Brian Williams, and Dave Anderson are all young players who have completed just one season of professional ball. Amelung was signed as a free agent and is an outfielder with apparent good power. Williams was drafted out of high school on the sixth round, and may have gone higher had he not lost baseball eligibility as a senior, learning a lesson he says he'll never forget. Dave Anderson was a number one pick and had the added pressure of being the top choice. He had to learn right away that you can't bring your personal problems to the ballpark and still expect to produce.

All of these players have had to struggle with their own personal demons at one time or another, and they are still fighting the battle. They have had to learn what countless youngsters have learned for years and years. Being a major league baseball player isn't easy. It takes enormous physical skills, but also the right kind of attitude and mental toughness, the kind of intangible that sometimes allows the less naturally gifted player to find more success than the so-called naturals.

At any rate, these eight ballplayers represent a very small percentage of the youngsters trying to make it all over the country, those still playing in high schools and colleges, and those in the minor leagues hoping to find a home somewhere, as long as it's in the big leagues. And from their struggles without a doubt will emerge the *Baseball Stars of Tomorrow*.

THE ORGANIZATION

It's no secret that the Dodger organization is one of the most successful in the big leagues. The team has had a succession of top talent since the late 1940s, and with the exception of a few down seasons, they have been at or near the top the majority of the time, first in Brooklyn, and then in Los Angeles.

The man in charge of the team's minor league operation is William P. Schweppe. Bill Schweppe has been with the Dodgers for 36 years and has been Director of Minor League Operations since 1968. He began with the organization as business manager of the Newport News Dodgers of the Class B Piedmont League in 1946, then worked around the minors until the team moved to Los Angeles in 1957. At that time he came into the front office, working with longtime executive Fresco Thompson, who ran the minor league operation, and in 1968 he succeeded Thompson. Bill says that it's this kind of long term continuity that has kept the Dodgers successful.

"This kind of continuity seems to be a hallmark of the Dodgers," he said. "Branch Rickey operated the club for a good number of years, then Walter O'Malley took over, and now his son, Peter, is in charge. And there is that same kind of continuity in the field. Both Al Campanis (the general manager) and myself have been with the organization for years and years, Walter Alston was field manager for more than 20 years and now Tom Lasorda, who has come through the organization, is the skipper. So there's always been a feeling of loyalty and togetherness, of family. Sure, we have our disagreements, that's natural. But we don't have the kinds of changes that disrupt the running of the organization."

The purpose of Bill Schweppe's part of the organization is to develop talent into major league material. Today it is done with five minor league clubs in addition to the parent club. The Dodgers have a rookie team, the Lethbridge, Alberta, Canada, Dodgers of the Pioneer League; two Single A clubs, the Lodi (California) Dodgers of the California League and the Vero Beach Dodgers of the Florida State League; a Double A team, the San Antonio Dodgers of the Texas League; and a Triple A team, the Albuquerque (New Mexico) Dukes of the Pacific Coast League.

Bill Schweppe explained that there is no limit to the number of minor league clubs an organization may have. Some teams have as many as seven. There is a policy that each team must have a Triple A, Double A, and at least one Single A club. By having a rookie club and two A clubs, the Dodgers feel they are providing a solid base for their Double and Triple A teams.

"I wouldn't call five clubs ideal," Bill Schweppe said, "but it fits our needs pretty well. Maybe we should have another rookie club to provide a somewhat broader base. There are about 30 ballplayers on the rookie club and maybe with two clubs you could have a few more ballplayers and give more kids a chance to get in some innings. We have about 150 players within the organization, and 40 of them are listed on the major league roster."

BASEBALL STARS OF TOMORROW

It wasn't always that way. The reason a team carries just five or six minor league clubs is really economic. Bill Schweppe said that excluding the leagues in Mexico, there are now about 15 minor leagues in operation. At one time, in the 1950s, there were something like 55 minor leagues in existence, with anywhere from six to eight clubs per league. That's quite a dropoff and by simple mathematics offers considerably fewer kids a chance to make it to the majors.

"Times have changed," Bill Schweppe explains. "After World War II there was no television coverage, no air conditioning, not as many autos, not too many other sports at either the amateur or professional level during the summer. So in any community where they could put up a ballpark and lights, there was a minor league ballclub. There were also fewer major league teams then, so play in the minors was very, very competitive.

"But slowly the time came when the minor leagues could no longer support themselves. Teams and leagues began disappearing. They could no longer make money and sign their own ballplayers, sell or trade their contracts, and draw enough people to pay the salaries. It slowly evolved to a situation where the major league clubs began subsidizing their minor league teams. Naturally, they couldn't do that for a large number of clubs, so the minors were pared down even more."

Before all these changes came about, it was sometimes more beneficial for a player to remain in the minor leagues. For example, players in the old Pacific Coast League could often make more money than they could in the majors and former major leaguers often returned to the PCL when their playing days in the Bigs were over. That doesn't happen anymore.

"A league like the Pacific Coast League was isolated then," Bill Schweppe says. "There was no air travel like there is today. It was almost like a third major league. You didn't have the radio and the television coverage, so the only baseball exposure they had was right there. It was a good deal for the players."

Dodger Scouting Director Ben Wade learned about that first hand, finishing his own career in the PCL in the late 1950s and early '60s.

"The coast league was the best league I ever played in at that time," Wade recalls. "Any number of players were making good money there. I remember George Metkovich was playing at Oakland when his contract was purchased by the Pittsburgh Pirates. He was asked to take a big cut to play in the majors.

"At that time, too, the Coast League was the only league that was flying. We spent a week in each city, every Monday off. We played for six months and lived at home, because the majority of the players were from the coast. So it was a good deal. You played six months, there was no salary limit and you could make good money. A lot of players felt they were better off playing in the coast league, playing at home. The money wasn't all that great in the majors, so quite a few players ended up on the coast. They made good money and if they had a name there, they drew well in all the cities."

It's not that way anymore, but at the same time the minor leagues were growing to 55 leagues in the late 1940s, the Dodgers were laying the groundwork for their continuing successful organization. And the man who started it all was Branch Rickey, an astute, knowledgeable, and daring baseball man. Rickey was an innovator, not afraid to take chances. The biggest testimony to that fact was that he was the same man who dared to break baseball's so-called color line, bringing Jackie Robinson to the Dodgers in 1947 as the majors' first black player.

BASEBALL STARS OF TOMORROW

According to Bill Schweppe, Branch Rickey was also the father of the farm system, and the man most responsible for giving the Dodgers a solid base for their own farm system that has remained to this day. He began the philosophy of developing home grown players which the Dodgers have continued. While the philosophy itself has not changed, Bill Schweppe explained that the circumstances under which the philosophy operates have changed. Branch Rickey lived by the credo that out of quantity comes quality, but quantities such as in the '40s and '50s are impossible today.

"At one time we had 25 farm clubs," Schweppe says. "It was really a chore then, keeping track of some four or five hundred ballplayers. In fact, when I joined the Dodgers in 1947, Rickey had stockpiled a slew of talent. During the War you could take minor league rosters and expand them by putting guys on what they called the national defense service list. In other words, if you signed a guy and he went into the service, you simply put him on that list and he didn't count against your roster. So Mr. Rickey stockpiled them and then had tryout camps while everybody else was sitting around waiting for the war to end.

"When it ended, he had some six hundred ballplayers and they were shuttled down to Sanford, Florida, where they were sorted out and put on different clubs. That's when we had the 25 or so teams. Since that time we've tried to keep the farm system as strong as possible, no matter what economic conditions prevailed. Naturally, you're going to make some mistakes over the years, but I'd say that in the 36 years I've been with the organization, the Dodgers have been competitive, virtually in contention, in about 30 of those seasons."

Today, the Dodgers farm system continues to operate as a tightly run, closely watched organization. Bill

Schweppe and his staff oversee the development of every ballplayer from the time he is signed by the scouting department to the time he either makes it to the majors or leaves the organization. Mr. Schweppe is also in charge of the managers of the various minor league clubs, the coaches, and the instructors who do most of the teaching.

The majority of minor league players come from the amateur draft in June, when the high schools and colleges are graduating, and other college players become eligible for the draft, either after three years of school or at the age of 21. The high school players and some of the college players will start out in rookie ball and go from there. Some of the more advanced college players might start out in A ball, with a rare few beginning at Double A. Of course, with 26 major league clubs drafting in turn, most of the top players are taken after the first four or five rounds.

Years ago, before the draft, a team could sign a player as soon as they more or less discovered him. Now the clubs draft in order, so even if you are sky high on a player, there is no guarantee that you'll get the chance to pick him.

"There's no real sure thing when you're drafting players," says Bill Schweppe, "especially when you begin getting further down the line. Sometimes we do take ballplayers that are kind of borderline. We're admittedly taking them as longshots and occasionally one will surprise us. Then there are times when we need players at certain positions, such as catcher or third base, for example. In that case you don't always take the player of greater potential, but the one who can fill the need at that particular position.

"But by and large every player that we sign we feel at least has a chance to progress. Mathematics tell the

BASEBALL STARS OF TOMORROW

story very simply. There are 25 players on a big league team, and with more than one hundred others playing in your farm system, you know that not all of them are going to become major leaguers. So it's strictly a judgement call all the way down the line and you just hope you make mostly right decisions."

Bill Schweppe also explained that there are not too many trades at the minor league level. Most times when a minor leaguer is traded it's because he's included in a trade made at the major league level. According to Schweppe, the Dodgers make only one or two trades a year involving strictly minor leaguers.

Players can also be acquired as free agents and through the re-entry draft in December. There are also times when the Dodgers will sign a minor leaguer who has been released by another organization. In that case, a Dodger scout will have seen the player and recommend giving him a second chance. The team also occasionally receives letters from minor leaguers who have been released elsewhere. The letter might ask for a chance to come to spring training as a free agent or simply for a chance somewhere in the organization. If the team has a need for his position, they might invite him. But that's more or less a longshot, both for the player and the team.

During his 36 years in the Dodger organization, Bill Schweppe has seen changes in the young players who have come into the minors. He feels they are coming in with more sophistication, both on and off the field.

"By the time we get them today most kids have had better coaching at the high school, American Legion, and college levels than they had in the past. So they come in better versed in the fundamentals and with more real knowledge of the game. Off the field they are more sophisticated in that they have alternatives. Years ago the good athlete didn't always have a chance to go into other fields. Today it's often tougher to sign a good high school athlete because he can go to college. He's got an alternative. With the changes in the collegiate rules, a player can have it both ways.

"Take John Elway at Stanford University. He's already got a lucrative professional baseball contract, but he can continue to compete in college football and he's getting his higher education at the same time. That's what I mean by more sophistication.

"Most players still have the same kind of love for the game that the players had 30 years ago, plus they have the added incentive in that the rewards for success are now so great. On the other side of the coin, if a kid completes his education he can go out and get a job, say, in marketing, if that's his field and earn maybe $25-35,000 a year to start, plus pension plans, profit sharing, that kind of thing. So if a kid considers himself just another minor leaguer without any real hope of getting to the major leagues, he can opt for the alternative."

For that reason, fewer players hang around the minors for years and years, and few major leaguers return to the minors when their big league playing days are over. There are just too many alternatives.

And while the young players are more sophisticated, the entire minor league operation has also become more specialized and refined. There was a time, for instance, when each minor league team had just a manager, one man, and he did everything from pitching batting practice to sometimes driving the team bus. The Dodgers, for instance, now have fulltime coaches on each club to aid the manager. In addition, there are roving instructors who visit each team on a regular basis or when needed. The roving instructors are former major leaguers Chico Fernandez, Leo Posada, Larry Sherry, Jim Brewer, and Paul Popovich, along with Red Adams and Goldie Holt. It's a staff that has done its job well.

"Our players get all the workouts and instruction they can possibly handle," Bill Schweppe says, "so they are going to become better ballplayers faster. There is also much better medical attention available now, new methods for treating sore arms and other injuries. The ballparks and the equipment are also better and there's more of an emphasis on physical conditioning now. So the entire minor league operation is a more sophisticated one than what you had 30 years ago."

Another change that has gone hand in hand with the decline in the number of minor leagues has been an increase in college baseball, with longer schedules and a larger number of schools taking the sport seriously. With more baseball scholarships available (though they still do not approach the number for college football), more high school players are choosing to go the college route instead of signing right out of high school.

"College baseball is better than it's ever been, no doubt about it," Bill Schweppe said. "The sport may still not be a big moneymaker at the college level, but I think one reason it is doing so well is that the sophistication I spoke about has also affected the college programs. In fact, many of the men who played in the minors in the old days later returned to college and got their degrees. Some of them remained as teachers and coaches.

"So you no longer had the situation where the history teacher goes out there and throws the ball out and says, 'Ok, fellas, let's play.' There are more college coaches today who really work at it, try to bring out the best of the talent that's available. Some colleges now have maybe ten or so people on their baseball staffs."

According to Bill Schweppe, good college players signing a professional contract come in with skills somewhere between A and Double A ball. A rare few go to Triple A, but most start off at the Single A level. The major drawback, he says, is a lack of experience. Guys who sign out of high school and who have been in the minors the three or four years the other guy has been in college, have just seen that much more top flight competition and have had more opportunities to learn. But the college players can often catch up quickly.

Location also has something to do with it. Colleges on the west coast such as USC, or the Arizona schools play long schedules with some 70 or so games. But in the midwest and the east, where weather is a factor, a collegian may only get to play a handful of games in the spring and if he signs after that kind of schedule he's not going to be in top playing shape.

"Chances are, too, that a college hitter just hasn't seen enough good pitching, certainly not what I call the command pitches," Schweppe explained. "In other words, it's one thing to hit a fastball, but then you've got to take into account the location of the pitch. A college player may be able to hit a fastball that's out over the plate, but it becomes a different story when the pitch is in on him. A good professional pitcher is going to hit that spot consistently and he'll continue to jam him. So it isn't only the fastball, but the location of it, and better pitchers have a better sense of location."

But whether a player signs out of high school or college he still has basically the same road to travel if he expects to make it all the way to the top. For example, say a new player is sent to rookie ball at Lethbridge and plays perhaps 60 games there. That's when the process begins, with the coaches and instructors getting to know the youngster and working with him. Part of the manager's job is to fill out daily game reports and keep the front office informed of the player's progress or lack of it. Bill Schweppe is constantly getting reports from throughout the farm system and he talks to the various managers almost every single day.

The roving instructors also fill out reports on the players after spending time with the various teams. They, too, go back several times a year to chart the player's progress. If a player isn't making progress and seems to have the physical qualifications, the front office wants to know why. Then the next year, the same process of instruction and reports continues, with more concentration on weaknesses that were found the first season.

At the end of the regular season, a number of the young players are invited to the Instructional League, which is held in Arizona. The Dodgers have had an Instructional League team for 15 years now and there are about nine other organizations in Arizona and about 12 or 15 more in Florida, according to Bill Schweppe. Though there are ballgames against other teams, the main purpose is intensive instruction, where young players can work hard to develop and refine individual skills or areas of weakness. There is actually more time for individual, intense instruction during this period than during a regular minor league season.

Then, the following spring, all the players in the organization go to spring training at Vero Beach, where the Dodgers have one of the most modern, well-equipped facilities of any major league club. That's when decisions are made concerning not only the major league roster, but also to fill the remaining teams with the players best suited for each particular level of play.

"We have as many meetings in the spring as time permits," Bill Schweppe explained. "We discuss all our ballplayers and set up tentative clubs where we think each player will fit. There is a great deal of competition during this period, both against each other and against nearby teams. We actually start with the parent club, dropping the players off from the Dodgers to Triple A. Then when the Albuquerque roster is set, we drop everyone off to Double A, where we fill the San Antonio roster.

"We finally get down to the A clubs and then divide up the rest of the ballplayers, trying to give each team some balance. It's really a process of flow. They trickle down. Everything starts at the top and trickles down. Triple A gets the second choice and so on down the line. And, of course, there is movement during the season, either due to injury or to players performing above or below the level of ability we had projected for them. It's a never-ending process."

The Dodgers try to give every single player they have signed a fair and complete chance to advance and make it to the majors. But obviously there are many players who are not going to make it, no matter how hard and how long they try. These are situations that have to be handled carefully and hopefully with a great deal of sensitivity. Athletes egos are very fragile things, and young players in the minor leagues have often never before experienced the taste of failure.

"Sometimes you may feel a player no longer has a chance," said Bill Schweppe, "but if he wants to stay and play, and give himself another opportunity and at the same time we have a need for him, then we may keep him. But it's pretty much an individual thing. For instance, if it's a player of great potential who can run and throw, and do all the other things, but who has never been able to compete effectively, we tend to hold on to him longer with the hope that someday he'll be able to put all those good things together.

"Then, of course, there are cases where for one reason or another, the scouts simply made a mistake. They may have misread the player's physical potential. Perhaps the player simply leveled off early at a lower level because he didn't have the physical attributes to make him competitive."

Bill Schweppe has a policy of never releasing a player who has not been to spring training. In other words, a player signed in mid-season will never be released until he has a chance to compete at Vero Beach the following spring. After all, one of the scouts did see something in that player to sign him and by bringing him to spring training it's also a way for the front office to evaluate their scouts. So there is always a system of cross-checking and at the same time everyone is getting a fair shake.

Releasing a player is very difficult for Bill Schweppe. In fact, it's a difficult thing for anyone in baseball, because in effect, you're telling a man that he can't cut it, that he isn't good enough. But, as Bill Schweppe said, sometimes it's ultimately kinder to release a player than to allow him to continue to struggle.

During the 1981 season there were several stories written about Jim Buckner, the brother of Chicago Cubs star Bill Buckner. Jim Buckner was a longtime minor leaguer who always seemed very close, but never could quite make it to the majors. He finally gave up after about 10 years of trying. Bill Schweppe says he has seen quite a few players in similar positions.

"Yes, it's a case of a player reaching his potential at the middle level of the minors and there is no further place for him to go. Over the years you realize you're going to have situations like that. I can name a few players who had outstanding potential but never quite cut it. I don't always know where the reasons are hidden. Every organization has a few players like this.

"Surprisingly, perhaps, you usually release these players. This is a case where it's often the kinder thing to do, because the player often feels he's just a step away and he tends to try again and again, but he'll never quite get over that hump. Occasionally, one does. We released a player several years ago who wasn't going anywhere. Then he suffered an injury and that looked like it. But about a year later he signed with another club and now the White Sox have him on their major league roster and he obviously has a shot to play in the big leagues.

"In other cases, while releasing a player is a traumatic experience for him, he often knows it's coming. A player can usually tell when he's not making progress and other players are moving ahead of him. This is particularly true in an organization like ours which has been fairly successful. Guys always seem to know about where they stand."

With the Dodgers winning the World Series in 1981, the tinge of pride is felt throughout the organization. But it's a kind of double-edged sword. Being in a successful organization with the parent club the World Champs, the players in the minors know it's going to be a difficult road to reach the top within that organization. But the pride still shows, and that success is reflected right down the line, especially at Albuquerque, where the Dukes have won a pair of PCL titles in the last two years. So it seems as if the Dodger organization is continuing its winning tradition.

As to the future of the minor leagues, Bill Schweppe is certain that they are here to stay since they still provide the final training ground for future major leaguers. According to Schweppe, some minor league clubs today are owned by local businessmen or perhaps by some independent operator who feels that with major league

BASEBALL STARS OF TOMORROW

help he can still make a few dollars. It tends to be one or the other, said Mr. Schweppe. They can be civic minded people who just want representation in professional baseball, even if it's at the minor league level. They just want to be involved.

But the days of someone making a living by owning a minor league baseball team are pretty much over.

"There are a very few single operators at some levels who might still do it," said Schweppe. "They are very good salesman and promoters, and as long as we have those types it will survive. Otherwise, the major league teams will have to begin operating more clubs outright and subsidizing the others even further. But it's been pretty stable for the last ten years and, in fact, there is some trend now for the parent clubs to increase the number of minor league teams under them. But I think it will stay pretty much the same unless something radical happens within the economy to change it."

The minor leagues are obviously an integral part of the baseball scene, and the Los Angeles Dodgers have always taken their minor league system very seriously. Bill Schweppe has no plans to alter the basic principles Branch Rickey started so many years ago. Keeping tabs on five minor league teams, all the players, managers, coaches, instructors, and scouts is quite a demanding job, but Bill Schweppe and his staff have shown they are up to handling it. The successes of the Dodgers and their farm clubs through the 1970s and into the 1980s should be proof enough. They must be doing something right.

THE SCOUTS

Although the rules for signing new talent have changed somewhat over the years, one thing has remained constant. A baseball team and its minor league affiliates would not be stocked with players if it were not for the scouts. They are those solitary souls who traditionally beat the bushes looking for the next Willie Mays, the next Tom Seaver, the next Pete Rose. They go from day to day, hoping to discover him around the next bend, at the next ballpark, at the next meeting of two local high school teams from Anywhere, U.S.A.

Unfortunately, it's not as simple as that anymore in some ways. Yet, in other ways, it is. To begin with, the scout is indispensable to every major league team, each organization. And while he doesn't have to make the same kind of personal contact as he did in the old days, when it was a matter of first come, first serve, and the prospective player could pick the team, a scout still has to spot the talent.

The man who is in charge of this important part of the Dodger organization is Director of Scouting Ben Wade. Like so many others, Ben Wade has a longtime association with the team. He was a big, righthanded pitcher for the club back in the 1950s, when they were still in

Brooklyn. After leaving the majors he was one of those players who decided to finish his career in the Pacific Coast League. He joined the San Diego team in the PCL and eventually became a player-coach, handling the other pitchers while still active on the staff himself.

Up to that point, Ben Wade had not really thought about scouting, much less becoming one himself. It all happened rather suddenly.

"It was during the 1961 season," Ben recalls. "I was sitting in General Manager Eddie Lichman's office when the phone rang. It was long distance, and he kept saying, no, I can't think of anyone, but if I do, I'll call you.

"When he hung up, he suddenly turned to me and said, 'Ben, how long have you been playing ball?' Twenty-four years, I told him. Then he asked me how long I planned on playing, and I said that it was the only thing I knew how to do and as long as he kept paying me good money, I would continue."

That's when Eddie Lichman told Ben that the long distance call was from George Weiss, who was the new general manager of the expansion team, the New York Mets, which would be entering the National League in the 1962 season. Mr. Weiss was looking for someone to scout the Pacific Coast League and some designated players for the Mets. Eddie Lichman told Ben he didn't know of anyone more qualified to scout the league because he had been there for so long.

"He told me what I already knew," Ben recalls, "that my playing career was just about over. Then he suggested that scouting would give me a chance to get into another phase of the game. Good scouts were something every team needed. Up to that point I hadn't really considered it, but it was a chance to remain in the game. I had spoken with some former players who had become

BASEBALL STARS OF TOMORROW

scouts and they told me how much they enjoyed it, what a challenge it was. So I picked up the phone, called George Weiss, and began scouting for the Mets the very next day."

A year later, Ben Wade was in Santa Barbara, where the Mets had a farm team that happened to be playing Reno, then a Dodger farm club. He began talking with then Dodger executive Buzzie Bavasi. It was a time when almost all the major league clubs were expanding their scouting staffs. "I understood the Dodgers were putting on some more people, so I ended up leaving the Mets and joining the Dodgers," he said.

That was the beginning of a long association. Ben scouted for the Dodgers for 10 years, and in 1973 he was made Director of Scouting, his present position.

During his scouting days, Ben had an ideal setup. Lucky was the way he described it. He began scouting on the coast and remained there, covering the San Diego area and Arizona. So, in effect, he was always near home and totally enjoyed the experience. But Ben Wade is the first to acknowledge that all scouts don't have it that good.

"A scout leads a very lonely life," he says, "unless you're lucky enough to be somewhere like the west coast and scouting a big area like Los Angeles, where you can still live at home and go to ballgames nearby. When you have an area of approximately 100 miles, you can be back home every night. So it's great.

"But then take the scout who's in the east, the south, or the midwest. He might have to drive 400 miles to see a ballgame. He's by himself. He goes in, watches the ballgame, then goes to get something to eat. If he has a long drive the next day he might try to get some of it in that night. Sometimes he'll drive three or four hundred miles only to be rained out. Then it's on to the next stop.

"It's not easy now, but it was really bad, say, fifteen years ago when the scouts were beating the bushes to see high school and college games. Now it's a little better because there are better ballparks and the teams play more games, so the scout isn't as rushed to see a team at a certain time. Some of the colleges, for instance, play up to 75 games whereas they used to play fifteen. There are also more scouts and they're looking at more college players.

"So now a scout is more likely to meet friends, though they don't necessarily travel together. But they can meet for dinner and with more night games might be able to play a game of golf in the morning. But it's a rough job and the majority of the time a very thankless job."

Ben Wade says that the majority of scouts are ex-players, though not necessarily big league players, because teams can't pay a scout the kind of money big league players are used to making. Players today are looking for bigger and better things when they retire.

"That's why it takes a man who really loves to scout," Wade said, "a man who is dedicated, and has a very, very understanding wife."

But there are some advantages, too. For instance, a scout doesn't have to worry about being pushed out of a job by a younger man, as players do. As Ben Wade says, age doesn't have anything to do with it unless a man gets to the point where he can't drive.

"A scout of 55, 60, even 65 years old who is in good health and doesn't mind driving can be better than ever. He knows just what he's looking for. The way I feel, unless their eyesight goes bad, it's hard to beat good, older scouts."

And they are an absolute necessity. That's why Ben Wade has worked very hard to develop and keep the Dodger scouting system perking at peak efficiency. It's

BASEBALL STARS OF TOMORROW

the only way the parade of talent will keep flowing without interruption. The way it is set up, two-thirds of the Dodger scouts are fulltime employees of the team, and the other third are part time, working only during the high school and college baseball seasons.

There are 26 fulltime scouts in the Dodger organization. Ben Wade explained that the majority of them has at least one part time man working for him. Each fulltime scout has an area designated just to him and he has to answer for every single ballplayer coming out of that area, which is no easy task.

Some areas are more concentrated than others. For instance, there are five scouts working in southern California. Each has his own area and knows exactly which high schools, junior colleges, and major colleges he must cover. Yet in less populated areas where there isn't as much baseball, one scout may have to cover three entire states. That usually involves the smaller states and places where they don't play baseball year round.

Now the system begins getting complex. Four of the 26 fulltime scouts are what Ben Wade calls "crosscheckers." One is in charge of the west coast, another the midwest, another the east coast, and the fourth is located in the south. These men really have to hustle.

"The other scouts report not only to me, but also to the crosscheckers," Ben says. "They must alert us to every good player in their territory. The crosscheckers then must become familiar with every good prospect in his entire area. Sometimes I will interchange the crosscheckers so they can take a look at each other's prospects. And I still go out and see all the players I possibly can.

"That way, when we get to the June draft and begin talking about, say, a kid at the University of Wisconsin who seems to be a good prospect, we might already have three different opinions on him. If three different scouts have seen him and filled out reports on him there is much less chance of us making a big mistake. It doesn't eliminate mistakes, but hopefully pretty much eliminates the big mistake."

The purpose of all this careful work is to provide the Dodgers with the best free agents possible, including high school, junior college, and college ballplayers, a number of whom will hopefully work their way up to the big leagues.

"We would rather sign a player than trade for or buy one," Ben Wade explained. "For instance, we signed our entire 1981 infield of Garvey, Lopes, Russell, and Cey, and they've been together about eight years. Both our catchers, two of our outfielders, and seven of our pitchers were signed. Of course, you have to make an occasional trade, like for a Hooton or a Reuss, but basically our ballclub is made up of the players we sign ourselves. So we pretty much go along with what our scouts tell us."

Scouting has changed in that there is not the extreme personal contact with the players that there used to be. Before the present draft system, all the scouts would be competing for the best players in the area. So a scout would get to know the player, his family, his coach and even his friends. He'd have to sell himself and his team to the player.

"You don't have to do that today for an obvious reason," Ben said. "Your club might not even get a chance to draft the guy in the first place. But I do require each one of my scouts who turns in a report on a player to talk to that player or his family. He has to make contact with him simply to find out first of all if the boy wants to play ball, if he wants to continue in school, and what our chances are of signing him if we go ahead and draft him. I'd hate to draft a boy in the first five rounds and then not be able to sign him. Then you're just throwing away a draft choice."

One custom that continues to this day is the network of "bird dogs." These are people not on the books who tip off scouts to a hot prospect. Bird dogs may be coaches or just fans, and the tips can involve college, high school, or even outstanding Babe Ruth players. A good scout has to be aware of all the ballplayers in his area and the bird dog network can number in the thousands.

The majority of times a scout goes to a ballgame, he's going to see a player he knows about already. As Ben Wade says, a scout going to a ballgame in which he knows nothing about any player on either team can pretty much write it off as a wasted day. He's got to have a reason for going to a game. But if he's going to see a pitcher named John Smith, for example, he is also on the lookout for a prospect on the opposing ballclub or perhaps a junior or sophomore on John Smith's team that will give him a lead for the following year.

"You'd be surprised, but this is how you come up with the majority of your players," Ben said. "Nine times out of ten when a scout goes to see a player he'll see a junior on the same team who he'll think more highly of than the kid he went to see. Maybe that kid just hasn't improved from the year before. But that's pretty much the way scouting goes."

When a scout sees a kid for the first time he's looking for basic tools. In other words, how well the kid can run and throw? If he's a shortstop, does he have pretty good hands? Is he unafraid to swing the bat? If he's a pitcher, the scout is looking for a kid who can throw hard. Youngsters either have a good arm or they don't.

But the basics aren't everything. As Ben Wade says,

you're judging a kid on raw talent, what he shows you and what little can come from conversation, maybe a brief talk before a game if his coach allows it, or a quick chat on the telephone. That makes it very difficult for a scout to find the so-called intangibles—attitude, drive, mental toughness, the desire to improve.

"That's very difficult because the scout doesn't really get a chance to run a kid down and find out a whole lot about him," Ben explains. "If a ballgame ends at 5:30 at night the kid has to get dressed and go home for dinner. And the scout often has to get ready to drive to another ballgame the next day. So there isn't much time unless the scout decides he really likes the boy. Then he has to take the time to try to get to know him better."

A scout must also be something of a clairvoyant, trying to see into the future, and that's a very difficult thing to do.

"A scout has to look at a 17-year-old boy and picture what he's going to be like at 22 or 23," said Ben Wade. "If anyone could do that perfectly all the time he'd be working for himself and not a ballclub. There's no real way to tell how much a boy is going to improve. Other things can also happen. He might run into personal problems or start running around with the wrong group of people. Anything can happen after a boy signs and that is something no one can predict."

Though the basic tools needed to play the game haven't changed over the year, Ben explained that there is one ingredient much more important today than a few years ago when looking for minor league talent.

"All clubs today seem to be looking for speed. I'm not sure if it's because of the artificial turf or not, but I guess it started in the 1960s with Maury Wills and then Lou Brock. They brought back the stolen base as a potent weapon and caused other teams to look for more speed.

BASEBALL STARS OF TOMORROW

Now, everyone realizes that if you've got speed you can help your club both offensively and defensively. Slow men will clog the bases and won't get the ball in the outfield. So speed today is very, very essential."

Ben Wade also said that kids coming into the minor leagues today aren't really different than those from years ago as far as the basic talents and desire to make it is concerned. Some of them come in a bit more prepared because of improved coaching and playing conditions at the lower levels, the high schools and colleges.

"I can't say baseball isn't as good as it used to be," Ben said. "It is. But I don't think it's any better. They don't have better pitchers, for instance, than Koufax, Drysdale, and Marichal, guys like that."

Ben also explained that while his scouts might associate with scouts from other organizations, he doesn't want them divulging any information on prospects. He feels he should get all the pertinent information, not the scout's buddy on some other ballclub. After all, it is a competitive business.

"Why would I tell a scout from the Boston Red Sox, for instance, about how much I think of a ballplayer. Then three months later when the draft comes, Boston grabs that guy in the first round and we have to look elsewhere. So a scout can't afford to give out that kind of information. Some scouts do trade tips, so to speak, but I hope my scouts don't do it."

The scouting staff has still other duties besides going from ballgame to ballgame looking for prospects. One other way to find kids is to run a tryout camp. The scouts are free to arrange these tryouts whenever they feel it can be beneficial. Tryout camps are by invitation only, with certain designated players the club wants to see brought in. They are always high school players, and the team must get permission from their various coaches to bring them in. You cannot work out college players because of an NCAA rule prohibiting it.

At tryout camps the players are asked to run a 60-yard dash. They are also timed running from home to first. Speed, remember. Everybody gets a chance to field and throw. The pitchers have their velocity measured and are asked to throw a breaking ball. All of the scouts who happen to be in the area participate. Most times, the coaches and managers from the minor league teams are left out of this phase. As with everything else, there's a reason for that.

"Coaches and managers see mostly professional players," says Ben, "and as a consequence they might not pick up the same things from a free agent that a scout would. And the scout has to see so many professional games each year that he doesn't lose perspective. It's so much different watching a high school game than it is a college game. If you watch college games for two weeks and then go see a high school game, it doesn't look as if any of them can play. So the scout sees kids on all levels and can hopefully separate his judgements."

The Scouting Director also said that fewer players are being signed out of high school now than there were 20 years ago. Part of the reason may be the fewer leagues, but also more kids are going to college now.

"The colleges are coming up with better athletic programs," Ben said. "Now a high school player can go to school, play a couple of years and not only get an education, but maybe improve his game and come up with a better bonus two or three years down the road. Still, I find that the majority of really outstanding high school players will sign right away. First of all, there's enough of a bonus to make him want to sign and the outstanding player usually wants to turn pro as soon as he can."

There are also rules regarding the drafting of college

BASEBALL STARS OF TOMORROW

players. If a youngster passes up the draft out of high school or decides not to sign, and then enters a major college, he cannot be drafted after his first or second year. He has to wait until he's 21 years old or becomes a junior. If he should decide to leave school, he must remain out for 120 days before he can be drafted. So a player can't go to college, drop out the first of June, and be eligible for the June draft. He would have to wait until the January draft.

In addition, there is one other way that the Dodgers search for and find new talent. That involves players from the Latin American countries. There have certainly been many outstanding players coming out of the Latin countries in recent years, the latest being the Dodger's own young lefthander, Fernando Valenzuela. Since none of the Latin countries are part of the draft, the situation must be handled differently.

The Dodgers have two scouts in Mexico, one each in the Dominican Republic, Puerto Rico, and Venezuela. In all the Latin countries, except Mexico, it's the way it used to be in the United States. If a scout sees a player he likes, he's free to sign him right away. In Mexico, the major league team must buy the player's contract from the Mexican club he's playing for there. If nobody has him at the time, a Mexican club must sign him so that the major league club can officially buy the contract. So there's no such thing as signing a Mexican free agent, but Ben Wade feels that his scouts are always on top of the situation all throughout Latin America.

There is still another function of the scouting department, one which many people might not be aware of. That is scouting within the Dodger organization and within professional baseball. Ben Wade explains.

"We scout every one of our clubs during the summertime as well as every ballclub in baseball, both in the minors and the major leagues. This is a job for our full-time scouts once the high school and college seasons are over.

"The purpose of scouting within our own organization is to evaluate our own players, to decide which ones have the most talent and should advance the quickest. It gives us another way of crosschecking, another opinion. For instance, if one of my scouts looks at the Albuquerque club, his report may be entirely different than Del Crandall's, the manager. And I don't want the two of them getting together and saying the same thing. I want each one to tell me what he thinks of the player."

The scouts also cover other minor league teams and the big league clubs. They check out the minors so if a player is released by another organization they'll have a book on him. Also, they have to know because of the possibility of trades, and this is also the reason they are always scouting the majors.

"We also have scouts who follow the club ahead of us, the club we're going to be playing, or our playoff or World Series opponent. We want to know which pitchers are hot and which hitters are swinging well."

So scouting is a never-ending quest, a multi-faceted operation that keeps going all year round. If you need the minor leagues to supply the Bigs, then you need the scouts to fill the minors with the best players they can find. Certainly, the Dodger scouting staff has been one of the most successful around during the past decades.

All you have to do is look at the record, as well as the roster of the 1981 World Champions. Ben Wade already talked about the large number of players on the club who have come up through the minors. Some of the more recent products of the scouting system and minor league organization are catcher Mike Scioscia, second baseman Steve Sax, and pitchers Steve Howe and Bob

BASEBALL STARS OF TOMORROW

Welch. And there is also 1981 rookie sensation Fernando Valenzuela, who was discovered in Mexico. So as Ben Wade said, the scouts are on top of everything. What more could a team want?

THE STARS OF TOMORROW

Now it is time to bring the human element into the story. We have talked about the Dodger minor league organization in general, learned about its overall objective and the way it is set up, with everything running smoothly under the watchful eye of Bill Schweppe. It is a well-oiled, highly-effective machine.

Ben Wade talked about his department and his men, the scouts who seek and sign the young talent. But what about the players themselves? Who are they? Where do they come from? What are their goals, their desires, their fears? And how do they fit the Dodger organization and the sport of baseball into the overall context of their lives?

Hopefully, these questions will soon be answered through an examination of the lives and careers of eight young ballplayers. Each one comes from a different background and has his own story to tell. Only their objective is the same . . . to play baseball in the major leagues to the best of their ability.

Dave Stewart

Theoretically, Dave Stewart is not a minor leaguer. In fact, he spent the entire 1981 season with the Los Angeles Dodgers, pitching short relief out of the bullpen. For his efforts, he received a World Series ring, and you can't do much better than that in your rookie year. But Dave did have quite a trek through the minors, and there were times when he felt the whole thing wasn't going to work out. In fact, he must have felt that right away, for when he joined the organization's rookie league team, he was promptly part of a dubious minor league record. The team lost its first 25 ballgames without a single victory.

Though he made it to the majors in '81, Dave's tenure in the minors has had a profound effect on him.

"I'm always going to be a minor league player at heart," he said, "because that way I will always have the initiative to work hard in spring training. I won't assume that I have a job, that it's just going to be there. I'm always going to feel I've got to go out there and earn it."

Today, the 6-2½, 205-pound Stewart is a strong-armed righthander whose eventual niche might be as a starter. Yet for years he was primarily a catcher, and had pitched very little when the Dodgers drafted him. But again, one of their scouts saw the potential. There was even a time when things weren't going well in the minors that a discouraged Dave Stewart asked about the possibility of becoming a catcher again. The answer he got was short and simple. Sure, you can become a catcher, but you'll have to find another organization first.

So Dave remained a pitcher, and now it's beginning to look as if his hard work is finally paying off.

Dave Stewart was born in Oakland, California, on February 19, 1957. Nathalie and David Stewart had seven other children, but just one other son, Dave's older brother, Gregory. It was with Gregory that Dave first began playing ball. He was just seven or eight then and the two boys used to throw a ball around. It was a football as often as a baseball. In fact, Dave remembers starting to play football first, then baseball, and eventually basketball, too.

Soon Dave was tagging along with Gregory to the local playgrounds. His brother was five years older, and he eventually taught Dave many of the basic fundamentals of the game. Dave says he never had an idol, even back then. Two of his cousins introduced him to Little League when he was ten for his first taste of organized ball. He was a first baseman-outfielder, big for his age, and a pretty good hitter.

From there he moved to Babe Ruth League, but at that time recalls himself as a rather mediocre player.

"There were a lot of other guys better than me. I was just kind of a fill-in and didn't start to excel until I reached high school. But because I was a fill-in I began catching a little then. The team had plenty of outfielders and an older first baseman, so the coach asked me if I wanted to try catching. I did, and I liked it, and I continued to catch right through high school."

Though Dave already had a strong arm, he had done

absolutely no pitching to this time. "It just never came up," was the way he put it. In 1971, Dave entered St. Elizabeth High School in Oakland, where he embarked on a four-year, three-sport career.

On the baseball side, Dave was primarily a catcher, though he did pitch one game his senior year. He was a good hitter and his batting average rose steadily, from about .300 his freshman year to around the .600 mark as a senior. The problem was that the team didn't win much. In fact, Dave recalls that in his senior year of 1975 the club was about 2-12 in league play and 4-24 overall.

"You don't have many scouts coming around a team like that," Dave says. "And because we were so bad, I really didn't think about a professional career, at least not consciously. I was basically playing for the fun of it and maybe to get a scholarship to college."

Though not even Dave's coach told him he had a shot at a baseball career, it turns out that someone was watching him after all. It was a man named Ed Jewell, and Dave remembers talking to him his sophomore year and having Mr. Jewell tell him he was a good ballplayer. What Dave thinks happened was that Eddie Jewell finally mentioned Dave to another man, who was a bird dog for the Dodgers. That might have been the link to his eventual drafting, but that's also getting ahead of the story a bit.

Dave does recall the one game he pitched his senior year. He should remember it. All he did was throw a no-hitter, though he lost it, 1-0.

"The funny part was that I was just a fill-in again," he says. "We had a very small student body at our school and only about 20 guys on the baseball team. So when we were hard up for pitchers at one point, my coach, Bob Howard, asked me to fill in. It's funny, because I liked catching and even then didn't want to pitch. But I went out there and threw just fastballs. I guess the no-hitter was an accomplishment, but we still lost the game, so I didn't get that big a thrill out of it.

"Nor did I particularly want to keep pitching. I liked the responsibility of catching, the fact that you got a chance to call the shots and were part of making decisions. You were always in the game. I did begin to do some pitching during the summers in Legion ball. I'd pitch one week and catch the next, though I still liked catching better."

The sport in which Dave was making the biggest impression was football. He was mainly a linebacker, and though he says he's not normally a hostile person, he enjoyed the contact and competitiveness of the gridiron game. Then, during his senior year at St. Elizabeth, he began getting football scholarship offers.

At six feet, 190 pounds, he must have been quite a player, because the scholarship offers were from rather prestigious football schools, among them were USC, University of California, UCLA, Colorado, and Michigan State. There was just one problem. Dave wasn't really keen on playing college football.

"The thing that made me wonder was a visit to Colorado. The average lineman there was about 6-5 or 6-6, and weighed 230 pounds and up. I really didn't think I could compete on the college level, at least not as a linebacker. The problem was that it was a way for me to go to college. To be honest about it, it would have been a free ride. But I didn't think I wanted to go if it meant playing football."

Dave began playing Legion ball in Oakland again where one of his teammates then was Rickey Henderson, now a star outfielder for the Oakland A's. He continued to think about his decision, and when the

University of California coaches told him they planned to move him to defensive back, he reconsidered and decided to accept their scholarship. As a defensive back, he figured he might be able to compete. So in early June of 1975, he was beginning another season of Legion ball and working part time at a local Boys' Club. Then when he decided to accept the Cal offer, he started making plans to go down to Berkeley and begin a weight training program.

That's when he got the shock of his life. It was a Saturday and Dave was working at the Boys Club when one of his friends came in with a copy of the *San Francisco Chronicle*. He was all excited and quickly opened the paper to the major league draft lists. There was Dave's name as the 17th round choice of the Los Angeles Dodgers!

"I quickly ran out and bought a paper of my own," Dave remembers. "There it was, but I still couldn't believe it was me. I thought it was someone else with the same name. It also listed my position as pitcher, which could have been another reason I didn't believe it."

Dave's skepticism grew some more when a week passed and no one from the Dodgers contacted him, not even a scout. Maybe it was another Dave Stewart, after all. With all the ballplayers in California it was certainly a possibility. But shortly afterward, Dave received an invitation to a Dodger tryout camp at San Raphael.

"I don't know if they had any real intention of signing me or not at that time," Dave says. "After all, a 17th round choice is about as low as you can get. But I went to the tryout camp and both pitched and caught. A short time later a scout name Ron King came in with an offer and I signed. He was apparently the guy who was sold on me and got me the offer."

The Dodgers wanted Dave as a pitcher. He's still not

sure why, but feels the club didn't think he would hit well enough on the professional level to play another position.

"It was also a time when a lot of clubs were looking for good, young hard throwers," he said, "and I think I impressed them purely on arm strength. I was just 18 years old and I think they liked the idea of being able to mold a young guy who could throw hard. Sometimes when you draft a college player you have to try to change habits he's had for a long time. A guy like me they were getting fresh and they could teach me as they saw fit."

The excitement of the draft and the tryout camp changed Dave's attitude. When he realized he now had a chance to play professional baseball, he knew it was something he wanted to do. He was pleased with his bonus, and also felt that if he pursued football, he would be dealing with a career that is considerably shorter on the average than that of a baseball player. So the decision was made. Dave was now a pro and reported to the team's rookie club, which was then located at Bellingham, Washington.

Rookie League doesn't begin play until late June, because most of the players are first-year men who were just drafted. When Dave arrived he and his teammates promptly embarked on that infamous, record-setting, 25-game losing streak. It wasn't the ideal way to break into professional baseball.

"After about three straight losses I just didn't want to pitch anymore," Dave recalls. "In fact, I wanted to go back to catching. Our manager told us to keep our heads up, that we were basically a team of high school kids playing against many clubs with mostly college kids. So it was tough."

The team kept losing and Dave continued to have his problems. Obviously, he didn't know that much about pitching. He had a good, live fastball, but he couldn't really control it. In some 79 innings of work that year he walked about 82. He didn't give up that many hits, but he still felt much of the time that he wasn't going to make it. At the same time, Dodger officials didn't really give him any sign that they thought he would make it, either. So he was pretty discouraged.

That's probably the reason Dave approached minor league pitching instructor, Ron Perranoski, and asked if he could go back to catching.

"He gave it to me straight out," Dave says. "He told me if I expected to continue playing professional ball with the Dodgers I'd better make plans to remain a pitcher. Otherwise, I could go somewhere else. He said again that they wanted me as a pitcher. And while I had always been a Giant fan growing up and had never liked the Dodgers, I decided I'd better get on the ball and try to learn to be a pitcher."

In 1976, Dave was returned to Bellingham. Players don't normally spend two years in rookie ball, but his inexperience dictated it. He had been a starter the first year, but this time he pitched relief and was 1-1 on the year and still having control problems. When asked whether he preferred starting or coming out of the bullpen, Dave expressed an opinion that has remained true to this day.

"I didn't have any real feeling about it," he said. "I just wanted to play. That's always been my attitude. I don't really care in what capacity I serve a club as long as I was on that club. Starting or relieving, it just didn't make any difference to me."

The 1976 season didn't do much to bolster Dave's confidence. He was sent to the Instructional League in Arizona after the season and didn't even get to pitch in any games.

"I did all my work on the sideline, in the bullpen," he

recalls. "They said they were working on my mechanics, that I had a lot of flaws in my motion and delivery. To be honest about it, I really thought I'd be released after spring training of 1977."

Needless to say, Dave wasn't released. Instead he was sent to Class A ball, to the team then located at Clinton, Iowa. Becoming a starter again, Dave suddenly began putting it together. He was 17-4 at Clinton, and even got the chance to jump to Albuquerque in Triple A at the end of the year, where he won another game. So his combined record for the year was 18-4 and it seemed as if he was on his way.

"I can't really say what caused the turnaround," Dave says. "Maybe it was a lot of prayers. Actually, my control was much better. I only walked about 60 in some 190 innings and struck out 155. I was trying to develop a curve then, but threw mainly fastballs and a change."

Then it was back to Instructional ball for more work on mechanics, and in 1978 he was sent to San Antonio in Double A, where he was 15-12 as a starter, working some 200 innings. He was also elevated to the major league roster that year and at the end of the season was brought up to the parent club for his first taste of major league action.

"I got there September 1," he remembers, "but didn't get in my first major league game until September 27. I relieved against the San Diego Padres, but it was just mop up. We were getting beat pretty bad that day, so I wasn't even nervous. But the experience gave me a taste of what it was like. It was different from San Antonio, different from any place I'd ever been. It really gave me something to work for, though I still fully expected to be back in the minors in 1979."

Though he was back in the minors, Dave was now pitching for Albuquerque and was just a step away from the Bigs. Starting once again, he leveled off somewhat, finishing at 11-12 for the year. Pitching at the Triple A level, where the brand of ball is improved, Dave feels he knows why his record wasn't better.

"It was simply a matter of not having the breaking pitch," he says. "I was still going along throwing mostly fastballs and an occasional change. But now I was facing better players, guys who had played in the big leagues and were back in the minors, among others. If you don't have something off speed to show them, you can't win. They would just sit on the fastball and sooner or later they're gonna catch up with you."

Dave had been working on the curveball all along, but it just hadn't come yet. He says he was very inconsistent with it. Some days he felt he was getting there, that it was working, but on other days it just wasn't there at all. It was this lack of consistency with the off-speed pitch that was his final barrier to the Bigs.

Yet he wasn't discouraged now. He felt that if worse came to worse, he threw hard enough that he could win with a fastball and good location. But he didn't quit on the curve.

"I've always been a gamer," he said. "I knew I'd keep working on the curve. I still had time left in the minors since I wasn't out of options, so I wasn't pressuring myself to get the curve right away. I was just going to let it take its own sweet time and come. And I hoped when I did get it that it would stay."

In 1980, the curveball came. Dave pitched some 224 innings and finished with a 16-10 record as the Dukes won the Pacific Coast League championship. In the final playoff series with the Hawaii Islanders, the Dukes lost the first two games of the best of five, but bounced back to tie it by winning the next pair. Dave then pitched the title game and whipped the Islanders, 9-2, going seven and a third innings in the process, capping a great year and raising his expectations for 1981.

"I knew I needed a big year in 1980," he says, "because I was now out of options, which meant if they wanted to send me back to Triple A again in 1981 they would have to put me through waivers first and risk losing me to another club. So I really wanted to have a good year and force them to do something in '81."

In spring training Dave pitched often and well. He broke camp, still with the big club, and went west to participate in the preseason Freeway Series with the California Angels at Anaheim. He was still there the day before the season was to open, but the team had yet to make its final couple of cuts. That's when he was told Manager Tom Lasorda wanted to see him.

"Tommy looked heartbroken when I went in there," Dave recalls. "He told me I'd have to go back to Albuquerque again. I was really stunned. Then General Manager Al Campanis also talked to me. Apparently it was between me and reliever Don Stanhouse, who had been signed as a free agent for a couple of million. And when it comes down to a guy making $18 or 19,000 and one making $2.5 million, you got to try to accommodate the guy with the big pact, because chances are you're going to have to pay him anyway."

Though shocked by the news, Dave was still able to think clearly. And what he did next must have really taken the Dodgers by surprise.

"I refused to go back down," he said. "I asked to be traded, not that I really wanted that, but I felt that after six years of minor league baseball I had learned my trade and could pitch for somebody in the big leagues. The way I saw it I didn't have anything else to prove at Albuquerque. I had had four straight years of winning in double figures and in the past two seasons was first or second in the PCL in innings pitched. I just felt I didn't have anything to lose."

Theoretically, Dave couldn't really refuse to go, because the club could simply suspend him without pay. But he was taking a stand on principle, and he felt it would force the Dodgers to make some kind of decision. By then, however, the last thing he wanted was to leave the organization.

"I was proud of being a Dodger and had enjoyed playing in the organization up to that point," he related. "I had also made many friends, not just common day friends you say hello and goodbye to, but friends I knew I could call at any time if I needed help and they'd be there. Plus the organization had always treated me awfully well. But I was really heartbroken when I learned I hadn't made the club and felt I just had to do something."

Whether Dave's refusal caused the club to think harder about its decision is difficult to say. They undoubtedly knew he was serious and undoubtedly didn't want to lose a pitcher of considerable potential, one they had invested six years into molding and sharpening. At any rate, within 15 minutes Dave got the word to stay put, that perhaps something could be worked out. And by eight o'clock that night, the club had decided. Stanhouse was out and Dave Stewart was a member of the Los Angeles Dodgers!

"I really don't know how much my refusing had to do with it," Dave says. "Maybe my luck just changed. For instance, if I had an option left I probably would have gone. But it all worked out for the best, anyhow."

Dave's role in 1981 would be pitching short relief. He was the righthander out of the pen in short situations, and young Steve Howe was the lefty. In the early going, Dave really pitched well, and, as usual, it didn't matter that he was pitching short relief instead of starting. He was just happy to be there and help the club.

In the second game of the season he relieved against the Giants and got the victory. Next time out he was pitching against the Phillies. In two innings he faced the likes of Rose, Maddox, Schmidt, Mathews, and Bowa, got everyone out and fanned four. His early success also allowed him to accept short relief without any qualms. The Dodgers were using him in important situations and he was producing.

It had to be a glorious year for Dave. It's no secret that the Dodgers won the National League playoffs in the strike-shortened season, then went on to defeat the New York Yankees in the World Series, four games to two. For the season, Dave had a record of 4-3, with six saves in 43 innings, and a fine 2.5 ERA. But something happened in the playoffs that almost ruined everything.

The Dodgers were playing the Houston Astros for the National League West crown in a best of five series, an extra series because of the split season caused by the strike. Houston won the first two games, putting L.A. on the brink of elimination, and the losing pitcher in both those games was Dave Stewart.

"I really felt I had let the rest of the club down," Dave said. "I had come in in similar situations all year, and earlier in the season I had gotten the job done. Now, in the playoffs, I didn't get it down. I don't think it had anything to do with nerves. It was just my time. I made the pitches I wanted to make, my arm was possibly stronger than it had been all year, but I just wasn't successful. Fortunately, we rallied to win the final three games. If we hadn't, there would have been no one to blame but me."

So Dave survived that ordeal and it can only help him to deal with similar situations in the future. He thinks the Dodgers may want to try him as a starter in '82, but he also knows he will have to go out and make the club all over again, and that's fine with him. He is also extremely proud of his World Series ring, and says it has encouraged some of his former teammates in the minors.

"One of my good friends at Albuquerque, Tack Wilson, who has been in the minors seven years, came up to me and said, 'Man, I'm really proud of you because you stuck it out and you got your reward.' Things like that really make me feel good. Tack was thinking about hanging it up after one more season, but now I think he's gonna go a little longer and hope he'll eventually get his chance."

For Dave Stewart, the chance finally came, but not before there had been a lot of hard work and frustration, and one dramatic stand when he told the club, I'm ready. He still cherishes his minor league experience for the friends he's made and the lessons he's learned.

"Being in the minor leagues for so long has taught me that you just can't rush things in life. There are some things you have to wait on. There are going to be a lot of things that aren't gonna happen as fast as you want. But there's no remedy like patience. Be patient and nine times out of ten whatever you're waiting for will come to you, some way, in some form.

"My aspiration when I started playing was to be in the big leagues in two years. I really felt I could be there in two, but it turned into six."

For Dave Stewart, it was well worth the wait.

Ted Power

Like Dave Stewart, Ted Power has had a long trek through the minor leagues, and he is looking to 1982 as the year he finally cracks the major league barrier. He is also a pitcher, a strapping righthander who has had to work hard to put it all together and at times has faced disappointment as well as a number of arm problems. He has also experienced some of the bitterness that often goes along with years in the minor leagues, and at times has had to kick himself hard to get his attitude back on the right track.

Like most big fastball pitchers, Ted also had to get his mechanics under control and work on developing a breaking pitch. His early development was hampered by the fact that his high school didn't have a baseball team, and he had to travel part way across the country just to play some competitive ball. So it's been a struggle.

Ted Henry Power was born on January 31, 1955, in the small town of Guthrie, Oklahoma, located some 30 miles or so north of Oklahoma City. He was the third and last child born to Raymond and Theda Power, and their only son.

Baseball memories go way back for Ted. He remembers playing on a sandlot in Guthrie when he was about six years old. He was younger than the other kids there, so while they were playing, Ted was having a catch with his father.

"My dad would take me out there and throw me the ball underhanded," he recalls. "I guess he was the main influence in getting me started in the game. He never actually played the game himself, not even in high school. He was a football player then. But he's always been a big sports fan and was willing to give his time to help me."

At about the same time Ted began playing some baseball he was also introduced to football and basketball, and he played all three right up through high school. By the time he was eight, he was playing his first organized baseball and a year or so later was in the Little League, where he quickly became a star.

"When I was growing up I was always one of those kids who was just a little bit ahead of the others. I was pretty big for my age and could always throw a little harder and hit the ball a little farther," Ted explained.

"Little League was one of those deals where myself and two or three other boys who were also ahead, did all the pitching. My parents have a scrapbook from those days and it's almost a joke because it's full of no-hitters and one-hitters. We played five inning games then, and one time I struck out the first 14 batters. Then the last one bunted. I threw him out and had a perfect game. That was when I was 12, I guess."

Ted also doubled as a third baseman and catcher when he wasn't pitching, though he mostly caught. He and another strong-armed boy just flip-flopped between pitcher and catcher most of the time. Ted says he's never been a very fast runner, so there was never a question of putting him in the outfield.

While Ted was growing and developing his baseball

skills, he was also developing something else.

"It was always hard for me to take defeat, especially when I thought I had done well and it hadn't done us any good," Ted admits. "I began to develop a terrible temper when I was still a small boy, and I can remember getting so darned mad that I'd just cry. It was my father who finally helped me control it. He convinced me that I couldn't always control the outcome of the game by my own performance and now I can channel that same strong desire to win into more productive areas."

When Ted was about 13 years old and in the seventh grade his life changed. The family moved from Guthrie to Abilene, Kansas. So Ted had to make new friends, which is never easy for young people in a new and strange place. But he adjusted and continued to play ball. The only problem was that the high school there didn't have a baseball team. In the spring in Abilene, Ted Power became a tennis player.

"There was a summer league in Abilene, but it wasn't too good, either," Ted recalls. "There was a good reason for it, though. A lot of the people around Abilene were farmers, and the boys had to work, they had to cut weed and do things like that all summer, so half the time they didn't even come to the games."

Though the summer league games in Kansas were fun, Ted felt he wasn't really progressing. So his last two years in high school, he returned to Guthrie in the summers, stayed with relatives, and played American Legion ball there. His objective at the time wasn't to necessarily play professional baseball, but he did want to go to college, preferably on a baseball scholarship, and he knew the Legion in Guthrie was heavily scouted by the colleges.

"There wasn't much professional baseball in the area of the country where I grew up, both Oklahoma and

Kansas," Ted said. "So because I wasn't really around it, I didn't think much about becoming a professional baseball player. I did idolize some players when I was a kid, mostly Yankees, guys like Mickey Mantle, Roger Maris, Whitey Ford, and Yogi Berra. I guess the big reason for that was that Mantle was from Oklahoma, close to where I lived. My dad was a big Yankee fan at the time and I think that probably influenced me, too.

"But the region that you're from can really affect your attitude and development. California kids, for instance, often think about playing pro ball when they're freshmen or younger. Their big hope is to be drafted out of high school. In my case, there was no possible way in the world I could have been drafted out of high school."

Though he wasn't sure what he wanted to do with his life, Ted knew he wanted to attend college and figured he could make up his mind when he got to school. He had set his sights on Kansas State University, but they never scouted him as a baseball player due mainly to his situation. He finally did get a small scholarship from Abilene for being the top senior athlete and then got an academic scholarship from the Grain Science and Industry to attend the Agricultural School at Kansas State.

By the time Ted entered Kansas State at Manhattan, Kansas, in the fall of 1973, he was strictly a pitcher. That's all he had done during the two summers of Legion ball in Oklahoma. Being on an academic scholarship, Ted would have to try out for the baseball team as a walk-on. He knew then he'd be trying out as a pitcher only.

Sure enough, he made the club as a freshman and had a pretty good year. He remembers his record that year as being about 5-2. But he had pitched well enough for the school to give him a half athletic scholarship the following year. Then he had his first setback. The team was starting to work out in early spring, and Ted had pitched just two innings of preseason ball when he fell on some ice, breaking his right leg and tearing ligaments in his right ankle. It was a serious injury, one that would keep him out for the entire season.

"The coach was so angry with me that he reduced my scholarship from a half to a quarter," Ted recalls. "But that wasn't the worse part. By this time I was thinking seriously about the possibility of playing pro ball. I knew I could be drafted when I reached 21, and since I hadn't pitched against any other Big Eight Conference schools as a freshman, I was looking forward to a big year with hopefully some scouts watching me.

"I guess the coach just wanted me to get some experience as a freshman. But going into my sophomore year I was highly regarded and expected to be the team's top righthander. Then I broke the leg and it all fell apart. It was a very depressing experience for me. I didn't feel like hobbling to class on crutches and my grades went to pot, and the leg had to stay in the cast for a long time because of the torn ligaments."

Perhaps in a backhanded kind of way the broken leg helped Ted, because it really made him realize how much baseball had come to mean to him. He said he couldn't wait to get back out on the mound, and during the time his leg was immobilized, he worked with weights to strengthen his upper body. When the cast was finally removed he waited about a week, then started playing summer ball. It turned into his best summer ever, and also a summer when he did some serious thinking.

"Now I wanted to sign," Ted admits, "and I also wanted to be picked in a high round so I could get some bonus money. I began thinking, too, more about school and getting my degree. I was majoring in physical education with a minor in coaching and began to find the coaching part of it very appealing. I feel I can relate to youngsters and could probably coach them. So it gave me something else to work for."

Determined to make up for lost time, Ted came on and had an outstanding junior year for Kansas State. He remembers his record as being 8-4, and he set a team mark for strikeouts in a season with just under 100, maybe 99, he thinks. It's not easy to remember all the stats from back then. He does recall setting another mark when he fanned 19 hitters in one game, and it was part of a doubleheader, so he got the 19 K's in just seven innings.

Ted was basically a fastball pitcher then. He had a small curve, but was inconsistent with it. So that real good velocity was what impressed the scouts. He hadn't talked to a single one his first two years, but during his third season scouts from the Royals, Dodgers, and White Sox all approached him. None of them really gave him an indication that he might be drafted, however. His coach, Phil Wilson, thought someone would take him, but not in a high round and he probably wouldn't be offered much money.

His junior year at Kansas State ended before the draft was held and Ted went to Dodge City, Kansas, to play semi-pro ball during the summer. He was also working out there and awaiting the draft.

"Would you believe I got the days mixed up," he said. "I thought the draft was held on June 5th, but it was really held on the 6th. So there I was on the fifth, hoping to get that call, and when it didn't come I figured I didn't make it, at least not on the first few rounds. Talk about someone who was down.

"Then the next day I got home from work and the

people with whom I was staying said congratulations, you've been drafted. I said, well, it's no big deal because this is the second day so it's got to be a low round. When I found out I was wrong I felt like an idiot. Here I am, wanting to be a pro ballplayer and waiting for the draft, and I didn't even know what day it was being held."

When Ted learned he had been the Dodgers 5th-round pick he was extremely happy. He was also pleased with the $14,000 bonus the club gave him for signing. Then he was told to report to the club's rookie camp at Bellingham, Washington, where he figured he'd be spending the rest of the 1976 season.

"It's kind of an interesting story," he recalls. "I got up to Bellingham, and as is often the case in Washington, it rained all the time. So for the first two or three days we didn't do anything. Then we finally held a practice inside a gymnasium and I was throwing batting practice to some of the other players.

"Well, the lighting in the gym wasn't all that good, so it wasn't real easy to see, anyway. Plus I was throwing hard and a number of guys couldn't even hit the ball. A couple of others actually broke their bats. Ron Perranoski was the minor league pitching coach then and he had been watching me. When I finished, he told my coach there was no reason to keep me there and I might as well be sent up to Class A. So after just four rainy days in Bellingham, I was sent to Lodi, California, and I stayed there the rest of the season.

"So, in effect, I skipped over rookie ball and the in-between A team, and went right to their top Class A club."

But this isn't the beginning of a Cinderella story. At Lodi, Ted came down to earth with a thud. He appeared in 13 games, starting five of them, and compiling just a

1-3 record. He had control problems, walking 44 men in 51 innings, and his earned run average was an unimpressive 4.59. On the plus side his great velocity accounted for 58 strikeouts. When he stopped to think about it later, he realized he was trying too hard.

"At the time I figured it this way," he recalls. "I impressed them with my velocity at Bellingham, so now that I'm at Lodi I'll really show them some velocity. The result was that I was overthrowing and had no control. Then when I did try to let up and get the ball over the plate, they hit it."

It was a very difficult experience for Ted. Like so many other young ballplayers drafted by major league teams, he had been pretty much of a star all his life. Pitching and winning, for the most part, had come easy. Suddenly, it wasn't easy, and that fall back to earth is often very hard.

"I had a lot of support from my family and friends," he says. "They helped me all they could, but I was still far away and on my own. I found it very tough not being able to just drive on home and see Mom and Dad, and have everything turn out all right. The whole thing was really kind of traumatic. I had done so well up to now and suddenly these guys were just banging away on me or I was walking them. In college most of the hitters were overmatched and would swing at anything.

"But I really didn't worry. I still thought I could do it. Yet the season at Lodi served to wake me up. It made me realize I wasn't that much better than everybody else. I was now a step higher and was going to have to work to get better."

It's not unusual for a young fastball pitcher to have control problems. Location doesn't come overnight. After the season, Ted went down to the Instructional League in Arizona and made the All-Cactus team. But while he was pitching well, he was also eating well. He went to Arizona a big guy at 6-4, 215 pounds. But by the time the Instructional season ended, he was an even bigger guy at 240 pounds. He had gained 25 pounds and by his own admission, it was fat. Still, he was throwing the ball some 94 miles per hour, so he wasn't too concerned about the weight. Then Dodgers' General Manager Al Campanis took a look at the big guy.

"Mr. Campanis is a real stickler on weight," Ted said. "He asked me how much I weighed and I told him a fib. I shaved 10 pounds. Then he made a deal with me. He said if I got back to my original weight of 215 I could come to spring training early with the big club. We shook on the deal. That's when I realized I had to lose 25 pounds, not 15, as I told him."

So Ted came home and went to work in a local mill. He dieted all winter and dropped 15 of the pounds. Then, a month and a half before spring training he left his job and began running four miles in the morning and four more at night.

"I got back to my original weight and was in the best shape I'd ever been in. When I got to spring training Ron Perranoski didn't even recognize me."

After spring training, Ted was sent to San Antonio in Double A, and he looked for a big season. But it didn't turn out that way. First of all, morale on the club wasn't good. It was something Ted hadn't experienced in pro ball before.

"It was a situation where a lot of the players felt they should be either at Triple A or in the big leagues," Ted recalls. "They weren't happy and didn't hide their feelings. There was always a kind of grumpy attitude around. The unhappy players were always talking, stabbing somebody in the back, blaming someone else for being there. So there was no team unity, no way we could really win. I thought I might have been a bit disillusioned about pro ball. It was only my second season and here were all these guys complaining about not being where they thought they should be."

All Ted could do was try his best. He was starting fulltime and seemed on the way to a good season. After 11 starts he was 5-3 with 60 strikeouts in 67 innings. His control was still a problem with 55 walks, but his earned run average was down to 3.88. Then Ted began experiencing elbow problems. The pain was severe and the doctor diagnosed it as a tear in the protective sheath around the ulnar nerve, which is commonly called the funny bone. It was a fairly severe injury.

"I sat out about 10 days, then came back and tried to pitch," he recalls. "I just couldn't. So then I was out five weeks. Once again I came back and this time I lasted five innings. But the pain was still bad and I had to come out. Since there were just three weeks left in the season now, the team suggested I pack it in, especially after Dr. Jobe, the Dodger's orthopedic surgeon, told me not to pitch for at least a month.

"So I went home, which was a lot better than staying around San Antonio with a weak arm while everyone else was playing ball. Plus I was really scared this time, because I could barely straighten out my arm. I couldn't even throw a piece of paper overhand. It was that bad."

It's not a nice feeling for a pitcher when he experiences bad arm trouble, especially for the first time and when he's still young. You can't help thinking that you might never pitch again, finished before you even get started. Ted could just hope the elbow would heal with no aftereffects, and when the Dodgers asked him to go to Instructional League again, he'd get a chance to test it.

"I never got in a game because I couldn't get my

breaking pitch over," he says. "And I didn't have much of a break on it anyway because my elbow would hurt when I threw it. The nerve sheath hadn't healed yet. The injury also cost me a chance to go to the Dominican Republic to play winter ball. It was my dream at the time because everyone said it was like paradise down there. Rick Sutcliffe went instead of me and he turned out to be National League Rookie of the Year. So it was really frustrating."

By the time the 1978 season rolled around Ted's elbow had healed, but his curve still wasn't what it should be and he was sent back to San Antonio. Once again he had a mediocre season, compiling a 6-5 record while shuttling between the bullpen and starting assignments. He also came up with tendinitis of the shoulder and missed three weeks. He began to realize that he didn't have the stamina to go more than 80 or 100 innings without running into arm trouble, and that winter he began working with the weights to build up his strength. The other problem during the 1978 season was one of attitude. Ted understands now that he fell into that same trap he had seen with so many of his teammates the season before.

"I was dragging my feet, not really helping myself to advance the way I should have been," he admits. "I could have done better and I could have learned more. We had a good team that year. But I thought I should have been in Triple A. I was like one of those guys from the year before. I was ticked off and I just kind of put myself in a shell and stayed there all year."

That's quite an admission for a young player to make. Not everyone even realizes they have a bad attitude and to admit it usually means they've learned a lesson. Ted wanted to play winter ball after the season, but there were no spots for him. So he went to Arizona again and finally got to pitch down in Mexico for five or six weeks. He said it was no big deal down there and he had a good time in the sun and on the beach.

In spring training the next year he was put on a major league contract, something that must be done by the parent club after three seasons or they risk losing the player. Ted had even asked several times if there was a possibility of his being traded, but the Dodgers kept telling him they had plans for him and that he wasn't going to be traded. But it must have been discouraging when he was sent back to San Antonio for the third straight season.

Before he went, Ted got into an argument with Triple A manager, Del Crandall, who skippered the Albuquerque team. He told Ted he wasn't ready to advance and Ted thought he was.

"I said something like, 'I'll show you; I'll be there.'" Ted recalls. "I was really bitter against Del and the entire situation. But maybe that's what he wanted to do, because it fired me up and after a month or so at San Antonio I was 5-1 and beating everybody. That's when they finally moved me up to Triple A."

Ted arrived in Albuquerque still determined to prove he belonged. He started out hot, winning five of his first six decisions, then he slacked off. A combination of tough luck and some poor pitching on his part finished him at 5-5 on the year, making it still another frustrating season.

"I could have done better there," he says. "I feel I blew it myself. It was frustrating because it could have easily been a much better season for me."

But it was coming together. In 1980 he was at Albuquerque all the way and finished the year at 13-7, his best season by far. He also pitched 155 innings without arm trouble, still had some control problems with 95 walks, but also fanned 113. After all the struggle, it was beginning to seem worth it.

"I also had a good relationship with Del Crandall. I started to understand and trust him. In fact, he made me realize that I was the one causing myself not to advance as quickly as I wanted. He kind of made me look at myself, kick myself in the rear end when I needed it. It was time to grow up."

The fact that Albuquerque won the PCL title made it an even better year. Ted pitched some winter ball in Venezuela after the season, but before he went down there he was married. Now he and his wife Karen have a baby daughter and Ted obviously has more responsibilities. Then in 1981 he began living up to everything—the potential, the responsibilities, and his job as a starting pitcher.

Albuquerque had a steamroller in 1981. The club was strong at every position, and Ted Power was perhaps the best pitcher in the minor leagues. He finished with an 18-3 record, striking out 111 in 187 innings and lowering his earned run average to 3.56. He even got his first taste of the majors in September, appearing in five games for the Dodgers, starting a pair, and finishing at 1-3. But his ERA was 3.21. He pitched in a little tough luck.

"I was the starting pitcher against Houston when Nolan Ryan threw the fifth no-hitter of his career," Ted says, with a laugh. "Not much I could do about that. I was a little nervous at first, but I felt I pitched well. It was good experience and it's got to help me next year."

As for next year, Ted feels he is ready for the majors, both physically and emotionally. He is also out of options, so if the club wants to send him down they'll have to put him on waivers first. With his 1981 record at Albuquerque, it's a safe bet someone would pick him up. So Ted feels there's a good chance his address will be Los Angeles in 1982.

Ted Power has experienced both the good and the bad

in his minor league career. His advice for youngsters hoping for a career in pro ball is simple.

"Be honest with yourself," he says. "Don't disillusion yourself to thinking you're better than you really are. You've got to improve yourself. I went into it thinking I'd be in the big leagues within three years. I didn't make it, but I know now that I wasn't ready in three years. I didn't understand everything that was needed to play major league baseball. It took me a few years to learn, and that's when I finally made my improvement. Now I'm ready. I've learned to handle setbacks and I've also developed a faith in God that I didn't have before. That helps, too, because it takes a lot of the pressure off."

Pressure. That could be the key word. Like other minor leaguers on the brink of making it, Ted Power has learned to handle all the pressures, and hopefully the pressures to come.

Jack Perconte

Professional baseball has been a battle for Jack Perconte. He's not a big man physically, standing 5-9½ and weighing just 165 pounds. He was drafted as a second baseman, a position usually filled in pro ball by converting another infielder or an outfielder. He has had difficulty with his arm and his fielding, but not with his heart. Yet at the end of the 1981 season, Jack Perconte was 27 years old and beginning to feel that time was running out.

"I feel as if I'm old for where I'm at now," Jack said, after completing his third season at Albuquerque. "There aren't too many older guys in the minors and I'm at the point where my age is going to work against me. I really feel I've got to be in the major leagues next year. If I'm not, well, I don't even want to think about that. As far as I'm concerned I expect to be playing second base in the big leagues for someone on opening day."

There are going to be a lot of people pulling for Jack Perconte—his wife, his family, his friends, his teammates and former teammates. Not that Jack is any kind of charity case. He's a hustling ballplayer who has worked on all the individual skills during his tenure in the minors. And he's always had a strong bat, capped by a fine, .346 average at Albuquerque last year. That's stickin'.

Jack Perconte was born on August 31, 1954, in Joliet, Illinois. His father, Jack, was a machinist for U.S. Steel for 39 years and is now retired. He and his wife, Mary also have two daughters, Jeanne and Marilyn.

Like most ballplayers, Jack started at an early age. He remembers when he was five or six years old, going over to a big field not far from his home. There was a Pee Wee League game there and Jack walked up to the coach and asked to play. He was sent out to left field for his first taste of baseball action. He doesn't even remember how he knew there was a game there.

Jack also got some early help from his father, who had done some coaching at the Little League level.

"Around my area we played all the sports growing up," Jack said. "And anytime I wanted to go out and play catch, my dad was ready. I can remember many times just throwing the ball back and forth with him on the street."

Organized ball came early. There was a minor league to the Little League in Joliet and Jack was playing with the other eight and nine year olds, uniforms and all. He was a shortstop and a pitcher in those days. From there he went on to Little League, and when he was 12 led the league in hitting, showing that strong bat that would always stay with him.

He was playing the other sports then, too, football and basketball, but because he was always on the small size had more early success with baseball. There were no real idols or influences then, but Jack always had encouragement from his parents, who wanted him to play, but never pushed him if he didn't want to.

From Little League, Jack made the usual progression,

to Pony League, then the Colt League. He also began playing at Joliet Catholic High School, where he says he didn't stand out until his senior year, when he batted .434. He batted from the left side and threw from the right side. He still wasn't very big as a senior, standing about 5-9 and weighing just 150 pounds.

No one ever told him he was too small for baseball, but he ran into it with the other sports. He tried out for basketball his first two years in high school and just didn't make the team. Football he played as a freshman, but being small found the contact and hitting difficult. After that he didn't go out for football, which wasn't easy, because it was by far the most prestigious sport at Joliet Catholic.

By that time, Jack had a far-off idea churning around in his head, one he kept to himself, and would keep to himself for a long time.

"I guess like a lot of kids, you think about growing up and being a major league baseball player," he said. "It was kind of in my head, even then, but it wasn't something I'd tell anyone else about, because I thought they would laugh at me or something. So I just kept it inside myself."

Though he didn't have any idols, Jack admired sweet-swinging Billy Williams of the Cubs, a lefthanded hitter like himself. He was drawn to Williams' consistency and his mild manner. He also liked Bobby Murcer of the Yanks. But he still didn't know where his own career was going. He's sure he wasn't scouted in high school, admitting he was small and not pro material at that time. While he had good speed, he was already beginning to have arm problems.

"I had a good arm as a youngster," he says, "and did a lot of pitching in Little League and Pony League. But then it seemed as if I just lost it. I don't know if I wore myself out or what, but by high school, my arm was just average at best. I lost the pop on my throws and the situation got worse later when I was in college. It wasn't a sore arm, but it was very weak and didn't start to come around until I did some weight work in college."

Of course, not being scouted in high school didn't really bother Jack then, though his far away pipe dream remained. But now he had to make plans for his future.

"Back in the early 1970s, you just didn't hear of too many guys from our area being drafted out of high school, even though there was good baseball around. It's not like California, where it happens routinely. So I always thought in terms of going to college. I didn't have any scholarship offers, so I decided to go to Murray State University in Kentucky basically as a student. I had seen the school when I played there in a Colt League tournament and liked it.

"I had a small academic scholarship, nothing athletic, but I went out for the baseball team as a walk-on my freshman year. I was a second baseman by this time, having played there all through high school, mainly because of my arm. Anyway, I made the team, played as a freshman, and the following year the coach offered me a scholarship."

Jack was always a good student, but wasn't yet sure about a career. In the back of his mind yet was baseball, and he admits it was his major goal at the time, though he still kept it to himself and he didn't know whether he'd ever have a chance to make it.

His freshman year he played behind a veteran second baseman who was a junior. But the next year the coach, Johnny Reagan, moved the second baseman over to third so Jack could crack the lineup. Until that happened, Jack had been thinking about transferring, because he didn't want to sit the bench a second straight year.

But he started as a sophomore and had a pretty good year, finishing with a .323 average. He says his hitting gave him more confidence, but he still didn't know if he should think about pro ball with any real seriousness. Then the following year both Jack and the team were outstanding. Murray State made the NCAA playoffs for the first time and Jack Perconte hit .404. In fact, the team batting average of .331 was the best in the nation, which gave the school some publicity. And Jack knew that big league scouts would be at the playoffs.

The playoffs were held at Mississippi State, and Murray was eliminated when it lost its first two games. Jack had hit well again, and said he wasn't at all nervous.

"Nervous in baseball is kind of hard to define," he said. "When you're swinging good you're not nervous; when you're not swinging good, you are. And I felt real good down there."

But Jack still had not been approached by any scouts. That summer he played in a collegiate league with players from all over the country. It proved a turning point for him. He was near the top of the league in hitting with a .348 average and broke the league record for stolen bases with 31. He was playing with outstanding collegians from Arizona and Texas. Playing and competing with some of the top guys bolstered his confidence, and the scouts were watching.

Back then, a player had to be 21 to be drafted. The following year, he could be drafted after his junior year of college, even if he wasn't 21. But Jack was ineligible, and that depressed him, because he didn't think he could duplicate his fine season. He went into his senior year with a bit of a negative attitude and sure enough, he didn't play as well. His average dropped to .331, not bad, but a far cry from .404. So his hopes of being drafted were not high. He began thinking about other things.

"I was majoring in sociology and minoring in accounting," he said. "I didn't have any specific plans, but was beginning to gravitate more toward accounting. I was actually thinking about coming back to school for another year to study accounting even further . . . that is, if nothing happened in the draft."

So Jack awaited the draft, which was held on three consecutive days. Day one passed, then two, and then three, and Jack still hadn't heard anything. His sisters were calling all the newspapers trying to find out if his name was on the list and everybody said no.

"My whole family was pretty down because they all wanted it for me," Jack said. "And I went to bed that Thursday night thinking I hadn't been drafted at all. The next morning I was still asleep when I heard my mom yelling, 'The Dodgers are on the phone! The Dodgers are on the phone!' I bolted to the phone and sure enough, the Dodgers had drafted me on the 16th round and they said they'd be over to talk to me about signing."

So in the summer of 1976 Jack's dream seemed to be coming true. He had graduated from Murray State with a B.A. in Sociology, but was still hoping to play ball. Naturally, he signed right away and was pleased to learn that he was being assigned to the Dodgers' top A team at Lodi. What he didn't know then was that his battle was just beginning.

Jack hit well right away, though he admits his fielding was a little below average. He wound up playing about half a season at Lodi and hit .286, with a homer, seven doubles, and 19 RBI's to go along with his 72 hits. He said he was over .300 until the final weeks when he tired because of not being used to playing so many games.

"The last two weeks of the season I could hardly get my bat around," he said.

After attending Instructional League during the off-season, he returned to Lodi again in 1977 and put together an outstanding season. In 131 games he batted .334 with six homers and 58 RBI's. He certainly didn't fit the mold of the weak-hitting second baseman, and he enjoyed the season even more because Lodi took the league title. However, he was well aware of his biggest weakness as a ballplayer.

"It was in the field. I improved somewhat, but didn't really make any major strides," he said. "I was an average infielder at best, and very weak at turning the double play. I knew that. We did a lot of work in Instruction League after the regular season and in 1978 I moved up to San Antonio in Double A."

Jack had some adjustments to make in Double A, where the level of competition was that much better. In fact, the first half of the season he had a real fear of being sent back to Lodi. No one likes to take a backward step, even at the lower levels. His hitting finally came around and he had a .275 season. He also swiped 46 bases, showing his aggressiveness on the lines. And he felt his fielding was coming along.

"I did a good job fielding the ball, everything except the double-play," he admits. "I had developed a kind of hitch in my throwing. I don't know exactly when it happened, but I just couldn't get rid of the ball quick enough. And if you can't make the double play it can kill you. That was the big obstacle I saw then."

Yet he seemed to be making a fast climb through the organization. In 1979 he was moved up to Triple A and was the starting second baseman for Albuquerque. So in three years, Jack Perconte seemed on the threshold of the big leagues. And at Albuquerque he found someone who vowed to end his throwing problem.

"From the first day of spring training, Del Crandall came up to me and said, 'We're really gonna work on your throwing. Everyday we're coming out early and work.' That's what we did. We started on our knees, about 10 feet apart, and he would show me how he wanted me to throw the ball. I'd do it over and over, and it felt terrible. I'd tell him that and he'd say to just keep doing it.

"We worked on it all during spring training and for two weeks at Albuquerque. Eventually we got further and further apart. He wanted me on my knees so I'd just use my arm, no other muscles, just basic arm motion. Believe it or not by the middle of the season I was throwing the ball really well. I didn't have the hitch any longer. I have no one but my manager to thank for it."

Jack really hit well the first part of the season and was still up around .400 on June 1. His throwing was better, but now he was having problems fielding the ball. He thinks it became a kind of mental thing because all his concentration was going to his hitting and throwing. In fact, it got so bad that he wound up setting a league record for errors.

He finished the season with a fine, .322 batting average and 68 runs batted in for 143 games. He also stole another 32 bases, and except for his fielding, still looked to be an outstanding major league prospect. But come 1980 he was again back at Albuquerque and by then he feels he had the rap of being a poor fielder. He had spent more time in winter ball after 1979 and worked on his fielding exclusively. So in 1980 he improved and still continued to hit well, batting .326 while swiping another

BASEBALL STARS OF TOMORROW

44 sacks. And this time he was part of a championship team.

The one additional thing that happened was his first taste of major league action. The Dodgers called him up after the PCL season ended and he got into 14 games in September, getting four hits in 17 at bats and stealing three bases. Yet he was back in Albuquerque for 1981 and beginning to wonder if and when he would get a chance to play in the Bigs.

Then in 1981 Jack Perconte experienced the good and the bad of minor league life. Albuquerque had a powerful team and rolled over its PCL opponents. Jack was playing the best ball of his life, hitting very well and fielding better than he ever had. But in August something happened that really made him wonder for the first time whether the Dodgers had any permanent plans for him.

Longtime Dodger second baseman Davey Lopes went down with an injury. When that happens, a club usually dips down to its Triple A team for a replacement. In this case, that would have meant Jack. But instead of doing that, the Dodgers brought up a 21-year-old second baseman, Steve Sax, from their Double A team in San Antonio. That's one of the most crushing things that can happen to a minor leaguer, to have someone jump over him just like that.

"It was a very difficult thing for me to deal with," Jack admits. "It was a real shock and truthfully, I didn't know how to act. All of a sudden you go to the park and everyone is looking at you and saying they're sorry, that kind of thing. It also affected my family and that really hurt. I had been married back in 1978, so I had a wife pulling for me as well as my parents and sisters.

"When I got over the shock I did tell Al Campanis

that I didn't think the Dodgers had any real plans for me, but he didn't really tell me anything. Playing for a team like Albuquerque really helped, because we were going so well and driving toward the playoffs. It seemed like the playing field was the only place I could get my mind off the situation.

"Del Crandall has always been honest with me and he said he'd felt for a couple of years that I could play in the majors. He kept telling me that I'd be there with somebody. But he also told me the other side, that things don't always work out and I should just keep my head up and do my best, which is pretty much the way I looked at it. But I did feel pretty sure that the Dodgers would trade me before 1982 began."

Jack finished 1981 in fine style. Albuquerque won the PCL again with Jack hitting a torrid .346, driving in 58 runs, and stealing 45 bases. He was up with the Dodgers again briefly at the end of the year, only this time it didn't mean as much. Steve Sax had played well as Lopes' replacement and now seemed to be the second baseman of the future.

After the season Jack talked about the possibility of an impending trade.

"I would think at this stage that if anybody does trade for me I would figure in their plans as a starting second baseman. In other words, they would give me every chance to see if I could play in the majors or not. Considering my age and everything, it seems they would have to have that in mind."

The incident with Sax in 1981 has also forced Jack to think a little more about the future. Though his goal has always been to get to the majors, he has always looked at baseball as a means to an end, not the final thing he wants to do in life. He's still not sure what he will do when his playing days are over, though he feels he would like to be involved in an area where he can help other people.

It seems to fit in with his overall lifestyle. His wife Linda has a career of her own and has been studying to become a Methodist minister. She attends Northwestern University and their schedules have sometimes kept them apart for up to two months at a time, which has been difficult. But as Jack says, they're both doing something they really love, and that makes it a bit easier.

Now it looks as if Jack is going to get a second chance. But he was right about one thing. It's not going to be with the Dodgers. In mid-December, Jack learned he had been traded to the Cleveland Indians in the American League. Since he had expected a trade, it didn't come as a complete shock, and he's now quite excited about the prospect of reaching the major leagues in Cleveland.

"This could be my break, a real opportunity," he said, "a chance to make the big club and play everyday."

He was told by the Cleveland officials that they want him as a potential immediate major leaguer and that they had been eyeing him for some time. He also feels the trade is good for his family, since they're located in the midwest and will be able to get to the games more easily.

The trade was handled well by both sides. Jack was told about it by Al Campanis and Tom Lasorda, and at the same time he talked to the Indians' Gabe Paul and Phil Seghi, their top front office people. So it was handled very professionally. The Dodgers wished him the best of luck and told him they felt it was a great opportunity for him. They also said that several teams expressed an interest in him, which also had to make him feel a lot better.

So it's been a rough road for Jack, but now perhaps

he is finally going to get there. He's gone through it all without becoming bitter or souring on the game. His advice for young ballplayers is simple.

"It's great to have a goal," he says, "but in reaching for that goal you've got to be sure you're enjoying yourself. I've always had a goal, obviously, but the main thing for me is that I really love going out and playing ball. The everyday game is what I enjoy the most. Hard work comes with the territory, but you've got to be able to have fun at the same time. In many ways, I've enjoyed the working toward it as much as the actual playing."

And perhaps at last, Jack Perconte's working and waiting will finally be rewarded.

Ricky Wright

James Richard "Ricky" Wright is a tall Texan with a blazing fastball and a desire to serve up his southpaw slants with the Los Angeles Dodgers. In just two minor league seasons he has moved into a position to possibly make the big club in 1982. But if he hadn't made a tough decision in 1977, he might have been pitching in the St. Louis Cardinals organization.

Ricky was one of many youngsters drafted right out of high school. The Cardinals were the team and he was tempted to sign. But that Texas Longhorn blood in him called and he decided to pitch for the University of Texas for a couple of years. Now he's glad he did it that way.

"If you sign out of high school you usually go to rookie ball or possibly A ball," Ricky says. "But I feel that while a player going to college may lose a couple of years of pro ball, if he's real successful there he is capable of jumping right to Double A, which I did. So for myself, I think I did the right thing."

Of course, there have been setbacks. All players have them and must learn to handle them. Ricky has had a freak knee injury and an illness, both of which set him back, but he's worked hard to regain the lost ground as a player must. He's also quite aware of how vulnerable a pitcher's arm and shoulder can be. One of his hobbies is shooting, both guns and a bow and arrow. A left-hander all the way, he's recently forced himself to shoot righthanded so that there are no extra pressures on his valuable left arm. Pitchers are like that.

Ricky was born in Paris, Texas, on November 22, 1958. His parents, John and Bettye Wright, had two other boys, both older than Ricky, Johnny and Kem. Ricky's earliest recollections of baseball center around his uncle, Larry Click, who once played in the Braves organization.

"Whenever we thought about Uncle Larry playing baseball we'd go out and play," Ricky says. "And when he'd come over we'd get him to take us out back and give us a few tips. I was probably just three or four when this started. I went out there and got the ball thrown at me, though I probably didn't catch too many then. I can also remember playing with a little red rubber ball, which we would cut in half so we could throw curves with it."

When his older brother joined a Little League team at age nine, four-year-old Ricky tagged along to watch. A couple of years later his other brother became batboy and after the games young Ricky would put on their uniform pants, tie them up tight with a belt, and run up and down the street.

"I thought I was in the big leagues right then," he remembers, with a smile. "But we had fun then because everyone in the neighborhood played. I can also remember afternoons, if nobody else was home, finding an old broomstick or a mop handle and going up the road picking up stones and hitting them. I hit many a home run that way back then."

Ricky was also beginning to play football, and later

some basketball. But Paris was primarily a baseball town and he always favored the diamond sport. He began playing Little League, where he was an outfielder at first and then later a pitcher. He was tall for his age then, but very thin, yet he made the all-star team his last three years.

From there he went to Pony League at age 13 and continued to pitch in earnest. He says he was big enough that he could throw the ball fairly hard, and that's what the coaches look for at that age level. Throw hard and throw strikes, and you can win. No one tried to teach him any other pitches then, not even a curve, though Ricky and his friends always fooled around with breaking pitches. In fact, he more or less developed his curveball on his own.

After Pony League he moved to Team League, then to Legion. In fact, when he was playing in Pony League at 15 and 16, he was already good enough to double up and play on a Legion team. And, of course, he also played at Paris High School.

He was already beginning to think somewhat about pro ball, especially when brother Kem was drafted out of high school when Ricky was a sophomore.

"I kind of started saying to myself, hey, when I'm his age maybe I can be as good as he is and get drafted myself. It really made me work harder. Sometimes the scouts would stay after the game to talk to Kem and I would be introduced to them. Some of them said they had seen me working out and thought I had some talent. Boy, would that kind of thing fire me up. I'd go nuts, and punch Kem on the arm going home, asking, 'Do you really think he meant it?'"

Ricky really began to blossom at Paris High. He was a pitcher-outfielder and in his last two years the team won the district title. He remembers tossing one no-hitter but says the real highlight of high school days was winning, and now remembering old friends and how happy they all were then.

"To be honest with you I'm what you call one terrible loser," he admits. "I always hated to lose, still do. Even my coaches in pro ball have to remind me that I'm not going to win them all. I was like that in high school and I always remembered something my Little League coach told me. He said somebody's got to win and it might as well be us.

"I know you've got to be able to take the ups and downs, but I've always looked at the winning side and failed to look at what might happen if I lose. I never did get along with people who said things like, 'Well, this is gonna be a tough game. I wonder if we can beat 'em?' My attitude is let's not talk about it. Let's just get out there and beat 'em."

So while he had a good time in high school, Ricky was already a very intense competitor. As a part time outfielder he hit around the .400 mark and there were even some people who felt he should try to be a full time player and not a pitcher. He was still flexible about it. If a team had drafted him and insisted he be an outfielder, he undoubtedly would have tried it.

He also played football in high school, but by his senior year of 1976-77 he gave up football to concentrate on baseball. Pretty soon he was going to have to make a big decision. He graduated from Paris High in May of 1977 and had scholarship offers to several colleges, including the University of Texas. Then in June, he learned he had been drafted by the St. Louis Cardinals.

"I almost signed with them," he says now. "It was one of those real tough decisions, the kind that after you make it you still wonder if it was right or not. But my brother Kem had gone to Texas instead of signing and

BASEBALL STARS OF TOMORROW

I had gone down there to holler for him a lot. I guess I had a bit of the orange blood in me by that time because I finally decided to pass up the draft and go to Texas."

So Ricky went to Texas in the fall of 1977 and that spring became a member of the varsity baseball team. He was hoping to get a fast start when he suffered his first setback.

"I was something like 3-2 in the early going and not doing badly," he recalls. "Then would you believe I just stood up in the dugout between games of a doubleheader and my right knee just collapsed on me? It was an incredible way to get hurt, but I actually had cartilage damage and had to have surgery, so my season was over."

Ricky bounced back quickly, strengthened the knee, and was ready to play summer ball in Colorado. It was a semi-pro league in Boulder, and he was with a team called the Baseline Collegians. He pitched well out there and helped his club win the National Championship at a tournament in Wichita, Kansas. Then he returned to Texas for his sophomore year.

The 1979 season turned out to be a good one for Ricky. He had a 10-3 record with the Longhorns and helped them earn a berth in the College World Series. The only problem was that he hurt his other knee right before the Series was to begin. This time he ruptured the bursur sac over the top of the left knee. He didn't need surgery, but he missed the World Series. Yet he was very pleased with the progress he had made.

"I felt things were starting to come together," Ricky said. "By that time I was throwing three pitches—fastball, curve, and slider, plus I was working on a changeup. Then it was time for another decision."

His brother, Kem, who had played at Texas for four years, had been drafted and signed with the Toronto

Blue Jays. Ricky, of course, was not yet eligible, but he would be when he turned 21 that November, that is, if he still wasn't in school.

"I decided that if I got a certain amount of money I would sign. So I took a chance. I dropped out of Texas, enrolled in Junior College back in Paris, and waited for the January 1980 draft. I figured if it didn't work out I could always go back to school. And if it did, heck, then let's go play some ball. It was what I really wanted to do anyway. It was truthfully the only reason I was going to school, because of baseball."

Ricky was a physical education major at Texas when he dropped out, and he admits now that he sees more importance in an education than he did then. His present plans include going back to finish someday, but he had just reached the point in the fall of 1979 where he wanted to play baseball.

By then, Ricky was a solid 6-3, 190-pounder, and with his assortment of pitches and good velocity, he must have looked attractive to a number of teams. It was the Dodgers who got him first, naming him number one in the January draft, which is known as the Secondary Phase. It didn't take long to work out a satisfactory offer and Ricky signed.

"I was very happy about everything," he recalls. "I had known some people who were familiar with the Dodger organization and everything I had heard about them was good. With some organizations you don't hear all good things. And since signing with them I have no complaints."

Nor did he have any complaints when the Dodgers assigned him to San Antonio of the Texas League following spring training of 1980. He had jumped right to Double A, which made him feel good about his previous decision to spurn the Cards and attend Texas. At San

BASEBALL STARS OF TOMORROW

Antonio he started very well, and during the first half of the season he was winning, his record around the 7-4 mark. Then there was another setback.

"I got sick right after the second half of the season started," Ricky said. "It was some kind of viral infection and it really knocked me for a loop. I lost a bunch of weight and didn't really feel strong the entire second half, nor did I play up to my potential. I kind of limped home at 8-10 for the year."

But it wasn't a horrid 8-10. Ricky had started 23 games for San Antonio, completing five. He threw 152 innings, fanned 127, walked 85 and had an earned run average of 4.20. He must have impressed enough people, because when the 1981 season opened he was assigned to Albuquerque in Triple A. He seemed to be making a quick trip through the minors and was already approaching the doorstep to the Bigs. But Ricky felt he was ready for the move. In spite of his illness in 1980, he says he learned a lot about himself and about pro ball that first year.

"I would have liked to have won more games at San Antonio," he admits, "but it took me awhile to adjust. I remember winning my first game there and saying, 'hey, this is no different from college and I won there.' But the next game was a real tough loss and then I lost the one after that. Then, it finally hit me.

"I realized you don't go after the first six hitters in a professional lineup the way you might in college where you can usually coast seven-eight-nine. In the minors the seven-eight-nine was like a three-four-five hitter in college. With them you have to go hard all the way. In college there were always guys you knew just couldn't hit one of your pitches. So you'd just throw him three or four until you got them over and struck him out.

"That was another difference between the college and

pro games. In the pros I don't try to strike people out until maybe I get two strikes on him. In other words, I got to throw three pitches to strike a man out, whereas I only got to throw one to get a ground ball. So I learned these things at San Antonio and had to kick myself in the rear from time to time so I wouldn't forget them."

Another big help to Ricky his first year was Ron Perranoski, the minor league pitching instructor then, and now the Dodgers' pitching coach. Perranoski didn't mince words when dealing with his young pitchers, especially when they were doing something wrong. But he always explained why it was wrong and what they could do to correct it. Ricky says that Perranoski helped him with his motion, his delivery, with certain pitches and fundamentals. And he was always there to help when a pitcher needed it.

At Albuquerque in 1981, Ricky was surrounded by a topnotch ballclub, and that didn't hurt either. With a ton of hitting support behind him, Ricky rolled to a 14-6 record with the PCL title team, adding another win in the playoffs that brought the Dukes the PCL championship. He also won a very big game that doesn't show up on his record.

"It was at the end of the major league baseball strike," he recalls. "The Dodgers were getting ready for the so-called second season and they brought us in to play them an exhibition game at Dodger Stadium. I pitched the fourth through the seventh innings and got credit for the win. We beat them, 1-0, before about 38,000 fans. I had never pitched in front of such a large crowd before and I was nervous. But it was fun. In fact, I'd like to be back there soon."

He might be. Ricky acknowledges that he has a shot at making the big club in just his third season of pro ball. He feels a lot of it is up to him. He couldn't play winter ball because of an inflammation of a shoulder tendon, and he won't be disappointed if he has to return to Triple A. He would rather pitch regularly in the minors at this point rather than sit the bench in the majors.

Ricky also credits the Dodger system of roving instructors for helping him advance so quickly. He feels the most important thing he's learned is concentration, how to focus in on what he's doing. But he's also learned many mechanical things, such as the release point of certain pitches, and positioning his body so that the ball can be released correctly. He learned how to make these corrections himself when he was a little off. These are things the average fan doesn't know about and doesn't consider when he's watching his favorite pitcher work.

In the off-season he didn't do much throwing because of the tender shoulder, but he did some weight lifting and running, just to keep things going, as he puts it. He also works in front of a mirror to keep his motion smooth. He still considers himself a fastball pitcher, saying he has more confidence in controlling its location than his other pitches. That's what he's going to throw in tight spots.

The thing Ricky misses most playing pro ball is more of a chance to pursue his two main hobbies, hunting and fishing. Always an outdoor person who loves the rural life, he has sometimes found the cities confining and finds a real need to get away from it all.

"I often missed what I call the luxury of being able to get out and do what I want to do as far as my free time went," he explains. "I often felt I was confined to a motel room or a city, which I get tired of very quickly. There were times when I just couldn't sit still and would just have to take off by myself and try to find someplace where I could either hunt or fish. The one place where I was content, though, was at the ballpark.

"There were times I would go to the ballpark at one o'clock in the afternoon for a night game for that same reason. I felt at home there. I might just sit around and do nothing, but I'd feel more content there than in the motel. To me, the ballpark is a different world."

Ricky does have a need for diversions, though. He says if he thought about baseball 365 days a year with the same kind of concentration he puts forth during the season he'd go haywire after awhile.

"The reason for that is the kind of pressure I put on myself," he says. "I strive to do things a little bit better. If I throw a three-hitter that means there's three men who got hits off me that I know I could have gotten out. So I always feel I can do better. When I walk out between those white lines I strive to do my best, and there's always room for improvement."

In many ways, Ricky Wright epitomizes the strong, silent Texan. Instead of riding tall in the saddle, he stands tall on the mound, ready to shoot down the opposition. And he explains his ultimate love for the game in a way you'd expect someone from Texas to do it.

"You have a love for your parents and then a love for other things in this world. And one of the other strong loves I have is for baseball. I'm as content and happy playing the game as I am when I'm with my parents, and I do love my parents dearly."

The way it looks now, it won't be long before Ricky Wright is taking that love of the game right to the major leagues.

Don Crow

A funny thing happened to Don Crow when he graduated from Davis High School in Yakima, Washington, in 1976. He was drafted on the 7th round by the Pittsburgh Pirates. No, that wasn't the funny part. In fact, it should have been the answer to a dream. The moment of truth came when the Pittsburgh scout showed up to sign Don and then asked him to report to Florida immediately.

"I found I couldn't do it," Don admits. "I wasn't ready to handle leaving like that. I had no experience with that kind of thing and I got scared. In fact, the thought of flying all the way across the country the next day scared me to death."

That's quite an admission from an athlete who wanted to play pro ball. After all, there are times when a second chance doesn't come along. But there are also times when a man has to follow his instincts, and as subsequent events unfolded, Don Crow realized he had done the right thing for everyone concerned.

Don is a catcher, another player who spent the 1981 season at Albuquerque and is just a step away from the big leagues. Getting behind the mask is something most young players avoid. It's a rough job. And though Don is a big man, standing 6-4 and weighing in the neighborhood of 200 pounds, he feels that catcher was the only position he could have played successfully, and he's very candid about the reasons why. In fact, Don is candid about everything, a straight-forward kind of guy who knows what he wants and tries to always stay a step ahead when looking at the future.

But there were tough times, too, hard decisions, such as turning down the Pirates, and a long battle to become a respectable enough hitter to play professional baseball. Donald Crow was born in Yakima, Washington, on August 18, 1958. His parents, Carl and Donna, had two other boys, his older brother Dean and younger brother Darryl.

Don's earliest recollection of baseball goes back to when he was in the second grade. It was the end of the school year and there was an announcement that any boys interested in playing on a baseball team report to a nearby field after school. Don was one of the boys going out. It was a team coached by the father of one or his friends and sponsored by the local YMCA. He was seven years old when he started and that same YMCA team stayed together until he reached the ninth grade, competing in a succession of different leagues.

The coach's name was Jim Davison and he taught Don many of the basic fundamentals of the game.

"It was nothing complex," Don recalls, "but Jim was very good about teaching us the proper way to play catch and warm up before going out to practice. He showed us how to field ground balls, how to throw, and how to hit. He gave us a very good foundation, got us off to a good start."

Both of Don's brothers were ballplayers, too. His older brother, Dean, began playing baseball about the same time as Don, but he eventually gravitated toward basketball. His younger brother also played right through high school and into college. So it was quite an athletic family and the three growing boys were usually busy doing something active. Don eventually began playing both football and basketball, and continued with all three sports through high school.

When Don first began playing with his YMCA team he remembers wanting to be a catcher. So did a lot of the other kids. He happened to have a good arm for his age, so he ended up pitching, and when he wasn't on the mound, playing shortstop. Still, he managed to mix a little catching in, enough to give him a taste and something of a feel for the position. By the time he reached junior high school he was getting tall, but wasn't very fast, so the coach made him a first baseman. He remained at first when he entered Davis High School and that's the position he played his first year on the varsity as a sophomore.

Don had a good year at the plate as a sophomore and seemed to really be coming on as an all-around ballplayer. But strangely enough, after that year his hitting went back, and he struggled for the rest of the time at Davis. Defensively, he was doing a good job. His junior year he got his first taste of catching, and by his senior year he was a fulltime backstop. He was also playing Legion ball at the time, but the Legion team had a number of catchers, so he played first there.

It was a strange kind of time for Don, or at least to hear him tell it. On the one hand, he often seems rather self-critical about his overall ability. Yet at the same time he was beginning to think about a possible career in pro ball.

"I think I just had a certain amount of athletic skills," he says, "and without having to work that hard I could do certain things other guys couldn't. I could throw better than a lot of them, for instance. But I wasn't overpowering and I wasn't a superstar by any means. But I was good enough to go out there and play adequately at the high school level."

That doesn't sound like a guy planning to go on. But rumors of scouts hanging around had him listening hard.

"I had some pretty good teammates who had been watched by the pro scouts," he recalls. "Rumors fly around and you listen. When I was a sophomore, for instance, someone told me a pro scout had said something good about me. That always perks your ears up, even if it isn't true. It gets you interested. I had always enjoyed playing ball and always kind of wanted to at least give it a shot. So that helped me to work a little harder. So I kind of got my first inkling my sophomore year that maybe I'd get a chance someday."

Don was also beginning to feel that if he was going to progress in the game, it would have to be as a catcher. Yet to hear his reasons for not playing the other positions, you would think he was again being rather critical, rather tough on himself.

"I didn't run well, so it was tough to play the outfield. I didn't hit with power, so that kind of rules out first and third base at a higher level. I couldn't play second or short with my build and speed, and I didn't want to pitch. That rules out eight positions. I had a pretty good arm and once I started catching I could see that I had to stick with it if I wanted to play somewhere else."

Because catching is such a rugged, demanding position, there aren't all that many around once you reach high school, college, and beyond. In this regard, Don has a good deal of encouragement from his high school coach, Dale Ehler, who had spent a couple of years catching in the minors.

"Coach Ehler had seen the workings of pro ball a little bit," Don explained, "and he said that catching was one of the best ways to move up to a higher level. Plus I enjoyed catching. You're in the game every pitch, which makes it interesting. To me, for instance, the outfield can be very boring. You just stand out there all day. When you're catching it's hard to lose interest because you're right there. There are responsibilities and physical demands, and that makes for a real challenge.

"There's still some of the old stereotype of the catcher, the short, fat, dumb guy who doesn't know any better and is stuck back there wearing the tools of ignorance. But in truth, it's almost the reverse. It takes a guy who can do some things, and can think, and takes responsibility to make a good catcher."

Don was about 6-2, 160 pounds in high school, getting long and lanky, not the kind of build usually associated with catchers. He said it presented some problems at first, problems of quickness and mobility, but nothing that couldn't be worked on and improved.

Then there was his hitting. That just wasn't getting better and the scouts generally look for guys who can crush the ball or at least hang out ropes consistently. Don wasn't doing either.

"I guess I hit OK," he says, "but I kept hearing about high school stars who hit .570, .600, and I had to struggle to reach .300, which I don't even think I hit my last year."

So Don finished up his career at Davis High. In addition to baseball, he had been a forward on the basketball team and both an offensive end and defensive back in football. He enjoyed playing, but doesn't feel he could have gone any further in either sport. At that point his immediate future was still a bit hazy. He had gotten a kind of feeler from the baseball coach at Washington State University, but nothing on paper. He also had a combination baseball-basketball thing at Northwest Nazarine College, but no real firm baseball scholarship. That's when the surprise draft came, the Pirates tabbing him on the 7th round.

"When I first learned about it I couldn't believe it," Don recalls. "I was sky high, so excited that I couldn't wait for the scout to come and talk, especially since I didn't have the baseball scholarship. Anyway, he came and the presentation that he made wasn't real impressive, at least from our view, my folks and myself. The scout kept saying how great things were gonna be, blah, blah, blah, but he wasn't getting down to what it was really going to be like. He didn't really tell us a thing, just how great the organization was. Then he sprung the topper on me, that he wanted me to leave for Florida the next day."

That's when Don really panicked. His mother was already upset, saying please don't go, while his father was trying to leave it up to him, but really pushing for college. What it really came down to, though, was that Don was scared.

"Man, I thought, I'm a 17-year-old kid who had never been away from home and here was this guy who wanted me to leave not next week, but the next day! It suddenly dawned on me that it was the type of thing I don't think I could have handled."

So Don said no to a chance that countless other youngsters would have jumped at without a moment's hesitation. But a combination of instincts and fears had caused him to decline. In many ways it was a very courageous decision. Shortly afterward, he learned he had a full baseball scholarship to Washington State, which was located just 200 miles from Yakima and was known as the best baseball school in the northwest.

"So I went there," he says. "I was on my own and it

turned out to be the best thing for me. It allowed me to learn how to handle myself, but in a kind of controlled atmosphere, a college setting. It was definitely a better situation than if I had gone to play ball in Florida."

So Don entered Washington State in the fall of 1976, joining the baseball team the following spring as a catcher with very little experience. He had caught just 30 or 40 games in high school and that was it. In his own words, he was very, very crude. As a freshman he saw very little playing time, getting in during the late innings of blowouts. He also played some JV ball and concentrated on learning more of the basic fundamentals of his position. He also got some help from Greg Chandler, who was a senior and the team's regular catcher.

The next year Don battled for the starting slot with another young catcher and they ended up sharing the position about equally. Don described it as an up and down season, one of learning, but under game conditions. He continued to have problems with his hitting which he said was rather poor. The team, however, was good, and went all the way to the Pac-10 finals before losing to powerful USC. Don did some of his best hitting in the playoffs, and that had to be encouraging.

By this time Don definitely wanted another crack at pro ball. He didn't regret saying no to the Pirates, but he hoped another club would draft him after his junior year. As a consequence he did just enough studying his first two years to stay eligible for baseball. He was taking business courses and has since become very serious about school, returning later to work toward his degree.

At any rate, after his sophomore year he went to play in the Alaska League over the summer. That's a semi-pro type league open to college players and a very good experience for Don. He had a job during the day and played ball almost every night. The experience of being in another place was also helpful to him.

"I was isolated up there, on my own more or less," he explains. "It was a period of growing up, learning what I have to do to take care of myself and straighten out my own priorities. I was much more prepared after going off to Alaska than I was coming out of high school to go off and play someplace else. It wasn't such a scary experience for me anymore."

It was a busy time for Don. After Alaska, he was selected to play on a U.S. Collegiate All-Star team that was going to play in a world championship tournament in Italy. So now he was really getting around. He was there for two weeks and hit better than he ever had in his life. Then when he returned to Yakima in early September he got married. He and his wife, Karen, had to hustle back to Washington State so Don could begin his junior year. With a wife and the responsibilities that go with it, he began studying harder and preparing for what would be an important baseball season for him.

He was the starting catcher his junior year and had a good season. His batting average for the season was .305, though he says he was disappointed with his .225 mark in Pac-10 games. Defensively, he had a fine year, and his arm gunned down many a runner trying to steal. When the season ended he was made a member of the all Pac-10 team.

As a junior, now, he was once again eligible for the draft and a number of scouts approached him to ask about his plans, whether he planned to turn pro or come back to school. Don admits that being married caused him to think about the money end of it more. Still, he waited to see if and where he would be picked. When he learned that the Dodgers had chosen him on the third round he was extremely pleased. This time he and his wife talked to the Dodger scout for a couple of hours and quickly made a decision. Don would sign and play pro ball.

"I had been pointing to my junior year and we agreed that if the money was there I'd sign and start playing. Once you're a senior in college you have no real bargaining power. You have to more or less take what they give you. As it turned out we got fairly good dollars, and another big factor that helped us decide that I was going to be sent directly to Double A."

So Don signed with the Dodgers in June of 1979 and then joined the San Antonio team in midseason. Once there, he had quite a surprising start.

"I joined the team on the road and I'm sure all the guys wondered how good I was coming in fresh from college. Of course, I didn't know anybody there. They gave me a roommate and I went to the ballpark that night to find out I was starting. I caught the entire game and the very next night the other catcher broke his ankle. So there I was, my second night on a new team and I'm about to start catching every game, like it or not."

Don handled the catching chores well, but at the plate it was a different story.

"The pitchers just blew me away," he said. "I couldn't even hit popups off those guys. There were adjustments to be made and I couldn't make them. Every night, it seemed, we were up against good pitchers, guys who could throw breaking pitches for strikes, and guys who all seemed to throw hard. It was quite a change from college, where I faced a hard thrower maybe once a week. Suddenly I was facing one seven nights a week. I didn't hit college pitching all that well anyway, and when I got into the pro situation I just didn't hit."

Don said he expected good players in Double A, but was a bit surprised that so many of them were so young.

Once again he felt his defense bailed him out. He was catching well and again cutting down a lot of baserunners. Fortunately, his manager at San Antonio, Don LeJohn, wouldn't let him get down on himself.

"He told me not to worry about my hitting, just to keep swinging and it would come," Don recalls. "And he told me I was his catcher and to keep playing good defense."

The last month or so Don's hitting picked up a bit, though his final average in 55 games was .192. What really got to him that first year was the grind of playing every night. College or high school players just aren't used to that kind of schedule when they first come into the minors. Don came in at about 6-4, 180 pounds, but by the time the season ended he was down to 170, and by his own admission, all skin and bones.

"That had a lot to do with my hitting, I think. I just was not strong enough to get the bat around well. Also, the climate in Texas was very different from Washington. When you get to the ballpark at 3:45 in the afternoon and it's still 95 degrees with high humidity, it's tough just going through batting practice. By game time you're soaked in sweat and it's a wonder I even weighed as much as I did at the end."

Besides the weather in San Antonio, Don and his wife had to adjust to the size of the city. Karen Crow was also from Washington. Neither she nor Don had ever lived in such a large city with close to a million people. They didn't have a car when they arrived and with things so sprawled out it was difficult just getting around and also difficult to make friends, especially for Karen, because not that many Double A players are married.

"We made some friends through a church in San Antonio which helped us get along," said Don. "I'm not a drinking or party type so even on the road I don't go out with the players much. There were a couple of other wives that Karen could sit with at the ballpark and visit when we were on the road. But making friends was a slow process and that might have had an effect on how I was playing."

After the season, Don went right to Instructional ball in Arizona, where batting instructor Leo Posada often worked with him.

"We still kid about it now because when Coach Posada first saw me at San Antonio he said I was just terrible. But he started to get me on the right track in Arizona. I was hitting more line drives and had about a .250 batting average. So there was some improvement. I've never been a very strong person and I have been working to build up my strength and hopefully increase my power. Of course, if you don't have the right kind of swing and get your hips through at the right time, you won't hit with power no matter how strong you are. I'm still not in synch as far as a power swing, but I feel I'm batting better."

In 1980 Don went to spring training for the first time and worked out with the parent club, which he says was quite a thrill. Again it was because he was a catcher. They always need some extra backstops to work with the pitchers. When the season started he was sent back to San Antonio. He had played in 17 games there and was hitting .229 with his first home run when the word came that he might be moving up to Albuquerque because Triple A catcher Mike Scioscia was shuttling back and forth between Albuquerque and the Dodgers.

But it all became academic when a foul tip broke Don's thumb, a typical job hazard of catchers. In fact, he was healing the persistent rumors continued. In fact, he was told that as soon as the thumb healed he'd be moving up. Then Scioscia came down again. Finally, about a week after he was activated he got the call. So in his second minor league season he was already at Triple A, and the big reason was because he caught.

"No question about it," admits Don. "When I first signed I was already about the fifth catcher down the line. There was a shortage of catchers in the organization and maybe that's why they drafted me. So I was really in sight of the big leagues right away, though I didn't realize it at the time."

Don reported to Albuquerque and played that very first night. It was the end of May when he was called up and he caught regularly until mid-July. Then Scioscia came back down and the two platooned for the remainder of the season and through the playoffs as Albuquerque won the PCL crown.

Surprisingly, Don's hitting picked up in Triple A. That, coupled with his usual good defense, kept him there even after Scioscia returned. He found out later that it was Del Crandall, his manager at Albuquerque, who insisted he stay because he was doing a fine job. He finished the season hitting a respectable .264 in 83 games at Albuquerque, with a homer, seven doubles, four triples, and 23 runs batted in.

Then with Scioscia moving to the majors in 1981, Don was the number one catcher for the Dukes as they swept to another PCL crown. Once again he showed improvement at the plate, hitting over .300 for much of the year and finishing at .286 with 54 runs batted in.

"I still feel I've got a little ways to go," he said, "but I consider myself a respectable hitter now, not just an automatic out. I've got confidence up there, something I totally lacked when I first signed. I've also learned a lot more about defense and Del Crandall has really taught me a lot of that, being an ex-catcher himself."

BASEBALL STARS OF TOMORROW

The situation for 1982 is still open. Veteran Steve Yeager shared the Dodger catching duties with Scioscia in 1981. But Yeager wasn't playing much and asked to be traded on more than one occasion. That was before he became a World Series hero. If Yeager goes, there's a good chance Don will take his place. If not, there may be another year at Triple A. But now he feels he can play and compete in the major leagues.

He also made good on his promise to return to school, completing his business courses and graduating in February of 1982.

"That was important to me," he says. "After all, you never know in sports. I could be traded, released, or maybe injured. And even a good career lasts only 10 years or so. So I've got to prepare for that day, and I think I'm in a position now where if I do very well in baseball I can take care of myself financially, invest wisely and be able to pretty much manage my own affairs."

So far, things have worked out for Don Crow. He's made some difficult decisions, but they seem to have been the right ones. He acknowledges now that if he had signed out of high school it could have been a disaster, maybe two or three years in the minors and then out of baseball. He wasn't ready then and he was smart enough to know it.

"I've grown up a lot," he says, "just by being out in the world and traveling all the time, living in different places. I've learned to take care of myself and my family. We have a two-year old baby boy, Timothy, and my wife is expecting a second child. Both my wife and I have become more independent and confident that we can cope with whatever comes."

As far as advice to aspiring young players, Don says simply that youngsters should not gear all their hopes on playing pro ball. It's very competitive and teams are most selective in picking their players.

"So many times hopes are dashed. Only a small percentage of those signed make it to the big leagues. As far as those who have talent, they've got to learn the fundamentals or they won't go anywhere. I know that's how I got there, and I'm still learning. It never stops."

Neither has Don Crow. He's come a long way from Yakima, Washington, and he's now hoping his next permanent address is in Los Angeles.

Ed Amelung

Ed Amelung was a championship athlete at a very early age. By the time he was nine he was one of the best at his sport and traveling all over the country to compete. He wasn't an outfielder then, nor a shortstop, nor a pitcher. In fact, the sport at which he excelled wasn't baseball. It was speed roller skating and young Ed Amelung was one of the best.

By the time he was 12, though, his true feelings were showing through. He gave up skating, not because he was tired of it, but because it was beginning to interfere with baseball, which had taken over as his number one and has remained that way ever since. Now he is embarking on a professional career which he hopes will land him in the major leagues.

Ed was born on April 13, 1959, in Fullerton, California, one of four children born to George and Betty Amelung. Ed has a younger brother and two older sisters. It was George Amelung who introduced his oldest son to sports.

"My dad got me into most sports," Ed recalls, "and I know I always loved baseball right from the beginning. They had three levels of Little League when I was growing up in Fullerton, the A's, the B's, and the major leagues. I can remember playing in the A's and B's when I wasn't old enough for the majors. I'd finish playing our games and then go over to watch the major Little League games. I was eight years old when I started and have played some kind of organized baseball every year since."

And there was still another sport that Ed was learning at the same time. Once again it was his father who got him interested.

"My dad would take me and my friends roller skating on Friday nights. They used to have races during the matinees at the place we skated. I didn't know about it at first, but one day I picked up a flyer that explained it and I told my dad I wanted to try. As a matter of fact my brother got into it, also, and he also dance skated with the girls."

By the time he was nine, Ed was becoming an outstanding speed skater, competing in age-group with other boys the same age. Speed roller skating is not at all like the wild and woolly roller derby that appears on television from time to time. It's an actual race on a flat track with three heats and then the finals. There are eight racers in each heat and nine in the finals. The track is set off by two pylons at each end which the racer must circle. There is no bumping or hitting. If you do that you're disqualified. Passing must be done by going around the other skater on a straightaway.

From age nine to twelve, Ed was heavily involved in skating and quite successful at it. There were workouts just two nights a week, but Ed skated every night, raced, and worked out on his own. He also did a lot of running then to stay in shape for skating. During this time he was also playing baseball, even basketball, but they were seasonal sports while roller skating went on all year round.

Every June, they would have the regional skating

championships at Bakersfield, California, and Ed won the title there in his age group four consecutive years. He then went to the finals in such places as Arkansas, Nebraska, Texas, and Oklahoma. Twice he finished second in the nation, so he was a lot more than just another skater. He was good.

He could easily have continued skating indefinitely because the sport goes all the way to senior men, where there is no age limit. In fact, the races get longer and longer, and the senior men actually have a five-mile race. When he was 12, there was another sport that was beginning to dominate his time and his thinking. That was baseball, and he realized it was time to give up the skating.

"I guess I simply had a desire to play more baseball," Ed says. "I always loved the game, playing it, watching it, and have never gotten tired of it. So I no longer wanted to spend all that time practicing my skating. I just stopped competing."

Ed was an outfielder and pitcher in Little League, and he would continue to shuttle between those two positions right on up into Junior College. He always hit well also, and finally decided he would have a better chance as an outfielder-hitter than as a pitcher.

Though small for his age in Little League, he nevertheless won a Most Valuable Player award, then continued on to Pony League and eventually to Buena Park High School in Fullerton. He pitched and played the outfield there, and was slowly growing to his present height of nearly six feet and weight of 185 pounds. The most rapid period of growth came in his final two years. During the first two he was only about 5-6.

By this time Ed knew he wanted to pursue a professional baseball career. In fact, he says he thought about it all the time and took many extra workouts in high school. He had no real influence then, nor did he know anyone playing pro ball. But he had many friends with the same ambitions and they would all work out together.

"It was inspiring to have friends who had the same dreams as you did," Ed says. "And since we all had similar goals we'd talk about it a lot and work together, which made things much easier."

Ed was a California Angels fan then and his favorite player was Jim Fregosi. He followed all the big league teams as much as he could, but obviously favored the Angels since Anaheim Stadium was just ten minutes from his house. He was also having a successful high school career at the same time, though the team as a whole wasn't good and they had a coaching problem his final year that didn't help matters, either.

"We had a veteran coach right through my junior year, but then he left," Ed explained. "My senior year we didn't really have a coach, just a counselor who supervised the program. So I didn't really get much help from the coaching end. I worked on my own to try to develop my own skills."

Ed was still doing quite a bit of pitching, and while the team didn't go to the playoffs, he once pitched a fine game against Savannah High, beating the powerful club, 5-2, and knocking them out of first place and a chance for the CIF title.

During that period, several big league scouts approached Ed's father and talked to him. Ed says they were all interested in him as a pitcher, not an outfielder. But the southpaw thrower and batter was thinking about the draft on his own.

"Sure, I would have loved it," he says, "but I wasn't drafted and decided to continue with school, not only for the education, but I really didn't think I was ready for pro ball yet. I still felt I was growing and wanted to develop physically some more. I had one scholarship offer from Long Beach State. Other than that, only a junior college coach contacted me. But I wasn't discouraged. I didn't really want to go to a place like USC or Arizona State anyway."

Ed ended up going to Santa Ana Junior College and it turned out to be the perfect situation for him. The coaches there, Jim Reach and Don Sneddon, were both outstanding teachers and Ed says he couldn't believe how much he learned from them.

"I've always wanted to learn," he says. "Even in high school, but there was no one to really teach me. At Santa Ana these guys were willing to spend the time and I loved it. I learned so much in two years that I couldn't believe it. Mostly fundamentals. For instance, there's a lot more to hitting than just going up there and swinging the bat. I learned about bunting, moving a man over, things like that. I also learned how to catch the ball on my throwing side and hit the cutoff man on throws. I got to work on a lot of the little extra things that I hadn't really concentrated on before."

Ed was also beginning to get stronger. He hadn't been much of a power hitter before, but his freshman year at Santa Ana he hit .315 with about five homers in 35 or so games. The next year he batted .440 with ten homers, and called it one of the best years of his life. By then he was pitching very little and doing most of his work in the outfield.

His sophomore year, the spring of 1979, he was one of the leading collegiate hitters in California and the scouts were beginning to come around to talk with him. The Angels had been in touch periodically and indicated they were going to draft him, but they never did. Now, however, he was aware that there was a chance he'd be chosen.

After the season he won many honors, including Junior College Player of the Year for the entire country. He was a first-team All-American and again the Angels called and indicated they would draft him. Once again, however, they didn't. Nor did anyone else.

"I think the reason teams shied away from me was because I had a hitch in my swing," Ed said. "The coaches had worked on it, but I felt comfortable at the plate and was hitting well and with power, so I didn't think there was a need to change. But the scouts seemed to shy away from it for some reason."

By now Ed had quite a few scholarship offers from major colleges, including USC, UCLA, and Florida, but he decided to go to San Diego State, a school that had shown a continuing interest in him and had a good coach. That summer, however, he went to play in the semi-pro league in Alaska and became the only player out of a junior college to make the all-league team. He hit about 10 or 12 home runs, he doesn't recall exactly, but things really seemed to be coming together.

Then at San Diego State in the spring of 1980 Ed's play fell off. He only hit about .285 and now realizes that it was caused by trying to please the scouts.

"They were constantly making it known that they wouldn't draft me because of my hitch, so I was working on eliminating it, trying to please them rather than playing the way I can play. I began pressing and it affected my hitting. I was really down that year. I always give 100 percent and I wasn't used to being unsuccessful like that. There were so many things going through my mind. Plus I had only six home runs all year."

The college season ended in May and Ed anxiously awaited the draft in June. Once more he was contacted by the Angels with talk of drafting him. And once more they didn't. Ed was disappointed, but he didn't stand pat. He returned to Alaska and had a really good year, hitting around .320. He then played in the BBC Tournament in Wichita, Kansas, in August, featuring the winners of the various semi-pro leagues around the country. He had a great tourney, hitting around .380 with six homers in eight games.

He was now talking to a few major league clubs. His coach in Alaska, Ben Hines, kept telling him about the Dodger organization being one of the best and during the tournament the Dodgers began showing a real interest in him. Ed was a free agent now and could make his own deal. Finally, the Dodgers made an offer. So did Toronto, Seattle, the Angels and the Mets.

Finally, it came down to the Dodgers and Angels and Ed picked the Dodgers, signing with them on August 14, 1980. He had finally become a pro. He didn't actually play with the organization in 1980, just worked out a lot with them. He went to spring training the following year and was sent to Vero Beach, a Class A team in the Florida State League. That's where he spent the entire season except for a few games at San Antonio at the very end of the year.

Ed started slowly at Vero, but came on strong as the year progressed. He wound up playing 136 games and hitting a solid .297, with eight homers and 75 RBI's. He had 17 doubles, an impressive 14 triples, and 22 stolen bases. Not bad for his first season as a pro.

His biggest adjustment was trying to get up for so many ballgames, something he found to be mentally draining. Ed says he was really running down at the end of the season, something that wasn't helped by the hot, humid Florida weather.

"I tried to take the advice of my coach from junior college days," Ed said. "He told me not to get too high when things were going good and too low when things were going bad. Because if you start worrying about things like that when you're playing so many games, it's going to affect the way you play."

But overall, he was very pleased with his play. He made the all-league team and received a great deal of encouragement and help from the coaches. He was also impressed by the fact that there was always someone there to help, whether you wanted extra batting practice or felt like shagging some fly balls.

During the off-season, Ed ran four to six miles every other night, worked in a sporting goods store, and lifted weights to increase his strength. He also kept his batting eye sharp by hitting out of a batting cage three times a week. It's hard for young players to accurately set a timetable for making the majors, but Ed has one in mind.

"I think if I play Double A, then Triple A I should be ready. I would love to play Triple A this year as I feel very confident about myself now. But I'll have to wait and see. I've heard that to make the majors you've got to score well in several categories—running well, hitting well, hitting with power, good defense, and a strong arm. I think I'm above average in all of them. I threw out quite a few guys from the outfield last year. I just have average speed, but I stole 22 bases in 26 tries at Vero. So I feel good about things."

There was one thing that bothered Ed after his year in the minors, and that was the way he was treated when he returned home.

"It's funny, but I don't like to tell people that I'm in the minor leagues," he said, "because when they find out they seem to make such a big deal about it. I guess there's always kind of been a mystique about professional athletes and people seem to look at me differently now. It makes me uncomfortable because one year at Class A really doesn't mean much. I have so much more to accomplish and I really don't want people to think I'm somebody special."

Other than that, things have gone well for Ed Amelung. He hopes he's taken the first step that will lead to a long career as a ballplayer. After all, he'd much rather be a Los Angeles Dodger than Fullerton's fastest roller skater.

Brian Williams

Brian Williams knew pretty much about the life of a big league ballplayer when he was still a young boy. That's because his father, Art Williams, had been a National League umpire for a number of years, and was often away from home. He had the same rough travel grind that the ballplayers had, and he often told his young son all about it.

That certainly didn't stop Brian. He became a ballplayer at an early age. In fact, he played everything, becoming a four-sport star in high school and really overextending himself to the point where it almost hurt his baseball career. But he was drafted by the Dodgers right out of high school before he had reached his 18th birthday. Now, with his whole future before him, he's beginning his trek through the minor leagues.

Brian was born on July 26, 1963, in Bakersfield, California. He has two brothers and two sisters, and all the kids had to pitch in to help their mother, Shirley, when their father was on the road umpiring. In fact, when Brian was born Art Williams was a pitcher in the Detroit organization. He had a shot at the majors until he hurt his arm and became an umpire so that he could continue with the game he loved.

When Brian was just six, he got his first introduction to a baseball. It was thrown by his older brother, Arthur, and it hit him square in the nose. Since his brother was already playing a lot of ball, young Brian often tagged along after him. He played his first organized ball when he was seven, in a league that preceded Little League. He played a number of positions, most often shortstop, and he joined the regular Little League as soon as he was old enough.

At McKinley Elementary School he began playing basketball and before long was playing football, too. He says he liked all the sports then. He had no favorite until he was much older, when he slowly gravitated toward baseball.

By the time Brian reached Little League he was well on his way to becoming an outstanding athlete. He was always big for his age and headed toward his present size of 6-2, 190 pounds, which he reached in high school. After Little League, he began playing in the Junior Baseball Association. He was barely into his teens then, but he was maturing quickly.

In the Junior League one year he belted 19 home runs in just 12 games, and he says he was already thinking about a career in professional baseball. At that time he was still playing almost everywhere—pitching, catching, shortstop, third, and the outfield. There was a time when his father urged him to stick with catching, telling him it was the quickest way to the big leagues. Brian tried it but quickly found it to be a disadvantage.

"I caught for one whole year," he recalls, "and I noticed that my legs were getting bigger and I was losing speed. I didn't like that so I quickly eliminated catching."

When he reached South High School in Bakersfield, Brian Williams had become one of the best all-around

BASEBALL STARS OF TOMORROW

athletes in the area. He became all-City in four sports—baseball, football, basketball, and track—and lettered in them all. He was a wide receiver and tailback in football, a forward-guard in basketball, an outfielder on the baseball team, and a high jumper and long jumper in track. It was quite a load.

During his high school years, Brian's game continued to mature. He was consciously trying to become a complete player, and he had the help of his father, who had left umpiring by this time, and his uncle, Autie Williams, who was a high school baseball coach. By this time he was sure he wanted to sign a pro contract and he always tried to put baseball first because of it.

Yet his baseball might have suffered somewhat because he was always doubling in track during the spring season. Brian explained that the baseball games were usually played after school and the track meets were held at night. Many a time Brian simply wore his track suit under his baseball uniform, and as soon as the baseball game ended, the athletic director would drive him to the track meet. He didn't even have time to eat in between. It was a physically demanding schedule.

"Usually my adrenaline level was way up after a baseball game and it carried over to the track meets," Brian explained. "There were days when I had a lot of running and sliding in the baseball game that my legs weren't up to their usual for jumping at the track meet. On days like that they really took a whupping.

"Occasionally, there were conflicts. One time I had to miss the Valley finals in track because it was the same day as the championship baseball game. As I said, baseball always came first."

Brian was looking forward to his senior year of 1980-81. He had a fine football season and another really outstanding basketball campaign. Then he got ready for what he thought would be a crucial baseball season, with the draft coming in June. But then Brian ran into an unexpected and shattering problem. He was declared ineligible for spring sports because of a poor grade.

"I always felt in some ways it was a big misunderstanding," he says, now. "But it took its toll on me. It was partially my fault, but I also had a teacher who had missed about three weeks of school and I didn't feel it was possible to get an accurate grade under those circumstances. Still, there was nothing I could do about it. I was out. I couldn't play."

Brian would never forget how it felt not being able to play. Later, when some of his professional teammates were talking money, money, money, he looked at things differently.

"Missing my senior year sort of made the money part of pro ball cease to be as important a factor," he said. "I found I just wanted to play the game. That's all that mattered in the whole world. The money will always be there, and I think if some of the other guys had to sit out a season they'd realize how much simply playing the game really means.

"The experience made me hungrier. I wasn't used to sitting around and I realized how quickly it can all end. Other players seem to want to get up there to make the money, rather than to play the game. But playing baseball is it for me."

After sitting out Brian must have wondered if baseball would still want him. He wasn't aware of scouts watching him as a junior because they didn't talk to him directly. In the meantime, he had pressure of another kind, the kind that comes from the college recruiters.

"I only had about five offers in football, colleges in California, but I had a whole slew of basketball offers, at least one hundred of them, and from some of the big schools like Notre Dame. I can't even remember most of the others. After awhile I asked my counselor to just hold them and not even give them to me. Playing four sports and then having all these scholarship offers come in also affected my grades and caused me to become fatigued. It all became a bit too much at the end."

There were also a couple of baseball offers and a couple that would have allowed him to play both football and baseball. But Brian had already eliminated college football because he had some back problems playing in high school. The saving grace came when the scouts began talking to him in spite of the fact that he was ineligible to play.

"I spoke with several scouts," he said, "from the Cubs, the Dodgers, the Blue Jays. They all said they were thinking about drafting me and that made not playing a little more bearable. My original thought was to favor Toronto, because they offered me a chance to go to college and play basketball, then play in their organization in the summer, like Danny Ainge. That sounded like a good idea at the time.

"Anyway, the day of the draft came and I was sitting at home waiting. I must have dozed off when the phone rang. I was kind of sleepy and I thought it was Toronto calling to tell me they picked me on the 16th round. I guess I didn't sound too excited or all there, because he told me again. That's when I realized it was Bob Bishop of the Dodgers and they had taken me on the sixth round. All I could say then was Oh, Wow! I was surprised I went that high. Then I was really excited, I don't think I slept for a week."

There was no doubt in Brian's mind that he was going to sign. He knew the Dodgers were a very talented team with a lot of good talent within their organization. He had originally set his sights on making the majors in about four years, and knowing all that talent was there kind of worried him. But once he was signed he put all of that aside and concentrated on playing.

The Dodgers assigned him to Lethbridge of the rookie league and he quickly became the starting centerfielder. He did well, though as the second youngest player on the team he felt a lot of pressure. Practices were long and hard. When he first arrived he found nine to five practice sessions very wearing, being used to two hour practices in high school. But he was learning a great deal.

"I found there was much more to the game of baseball then I even knew existed," he admitted. "Most of it was mechanics, of hitting, throwing, running. I had been a switch hitter since my sophomore year in high school and the Dodgers wanted me to continue with it, though I was a natural lefthander. So I took a great deal of batting practice, did a lot of hitting off the tee and got a lot of instruction from the coaches."

Brian also found that everybody at Lethbridge was starting together from the same point. "There are many talented ballplayers in the organization," he said. "So even if you were a big star in your own town, once you get together here there's no star. But I expected it to be that way because my family talked about it even before I signed, when they still thought I might go to college. No matter how big you were in high school you've got to put that all behind you. Now it starts all over again."

Brian seems ready to practice what he preaches. In an era of superstars, the player he admires most is Darrell Thomas of the Dodgers, a utility player who can fill in well at almost every position.

"I admire the man because he doesn't get all that much opportunity to play, yet he doesn't make a fuss about it," Brian explained. "And he has played every position in baseball. He may just come in late in the game for defensive purposes, but he doesn't seem to let that get to him. It's that kind of attitude that I try to copy."

But Brian did more than just caddy at Lethbridge. In 54 ballgames in 1981, he led the team with a .305 batting average, hitting a homer and driving home 22. He also swiped 11 bases. It was a good beginning. Still, he felt he could have done better.

"I think I was hitting in the .380s when I went into a slump and got something like three hits in 20 at bats," he said. "That discouraged me a little, but my coach, Gary LeRocque, said that everybody goes into slumps and I shouldn't let it get to me. He told me to just do my job and I'd come out of it, which I did. The coaches did that kind of thing all year. They tried to keep the pressure off us, telling us that it was a learning experience and they were just trying to make better players of us. There wasn't that kind of pressure to win."

After the season Brian went to Instructional ball and then returned home to work with weights and try to develop more strength. He's looking forward to the coming season, though he still didn't know where he would be playing.

"I just want to have a good season and try to hit with more power," he said. "I'm not a real power hitter, though I do hit the ball hard at times. Right now I'm a little too aggressive up there. I've got to settle down and wait on my pitch more. I'd also like to steal more bases, but these things will come with experience."

Brian Williams also talks of returning to school some day and perhaps going into juvenile work, helping young kids without families. But right now both the Dodgers and Brian hope that's a long way off. Brian should have a long career ahead of him.

Dave Anderson

When you're the number one draft pick of one of baseball's most successful organizations the pressure can be great. You're a guy who's expected to produce. Add to that the sudden onset of family problems at the very time you're beginning your first season as a professional, and you find yourself really up against it. This was what faced David Carter Anderson in 1981. The tall, rangy shortstop came into the Dodger organization as a highly-touted prospect. Playing his initial pro campaign at Vero Beach he had to overcome a number of obstacles to produce a fine first season.

It wasn't an easy task, but Dave faced up to the situation and was able to look at it objectively. The lessons learned should help him greatly in the future, the adjustments he had to make in one season will undoubtedly add to his character. Among the things he had to do was change from an aluminum to a wood bat, something that was unheard of just a few short years ago.

The story begins in Louisville, Kentucky, where Dave was born on August 1, 1960, the second son of Max and Martha Anderson. However, the family wasn't there long. When Dave was just two, his parents decided to visit his grandparents in St. Petersburg, Florida. To put it in Dave's words, they simply liked it so much, they stayed.

So that's where Dave grew up. When he was about six he began tagging after his older brother, Charles, and his friends when they went to play ball. He was too young to play with them at first, but pretty soon he was practicing with them. Then when he was eight he began playing Little League. A couple of years later he started playing football, and soon afterwards he added basketball. From that point on he played whichever sport was in season and slowly became a fine, all-around athlete.

From Little League he moved to Junior League and then Senior League, and when he was 17 began Legion play. All the teams were very successful and Dave got a taste of winning at an early age. He liked it. He didn't have quite the same success with his high school team. The squad at Gibbs High School just wasn't that good and always seemed to hover around the .500 mark.

Until he reached high school, Dave alternated between pitching and shortstop. Finally, in the 10th grade he decided his arm couldn't take pitching anymore and he then played short fulltime. Though he felt that baseball was his best sport, the glamour sport in high school was football, and Dave began concentrating more on the gridiron game.

"I was a quarterback and I felt I had a chance for a scholarship," he recalls, "so I began working very hard toward that. In fact, I had more success in football then, at least statistically, than I did in baseball. Looking back, I was little more than your average high school player, although I did make all-City. I think I hit about .360 as a senior, which in high school isn't all that great."

In football, though, he was racking up the numbers.

BASEBALL STARS OF TOMORROW

He passed for more than 3,000 yards during his three varsity seasons, throwing around 25 touchdown passes and rushing for more than 1,000 yards. But again, the team wasn't very good and Dave recalls that they had identical 3-7 records in each of the three years in which he played.

But he got his scholarship from Memphis State University. When he accepted it, Dave asked if he could play both football and baseball. They told him yes, but after his freshman year. Since he was on a football scholarship they wanted him at spring football practice his freshman year, and that would knock out baseball. After that, they said, he could play both.

It was the fall of 1978 when Dave entered Memphis State. He played Legion ball before going to school and hit about .500, so he was coming on strong. He went through the football program as a freshman, but was redshirted, so he would have four years of eligibility left. He then went through spring practice and didn't play baseball, but that summer he came home and hit .500 again in Legion play.

His fine play in Legion was getting him some feelers from other colleges that wanted him as a baseball player and he was actually thinking about transferring. That's when the Memphis State baseball coach got wind of things.

"He called me up one day and said he heard I might be leaving school," Dave recalls. "I said I was thinking about it and he said, don't worry, you come out next year and you're my shortstop. The guy had never seen me play an inning and had hardly talked to me my first year. Now he's telling me I'm his shortstop. It was hard to believe."

But Dave did return to Memphis State, and in his words got battered in football practice that fall and didn't play a down. Now he could wait for baseball. But there was another big event in between. At Christmastime of 1979, Dave was married. He and his wife, Gina, returned to Memphis State and that spring Dave went out for baseball. Sure enough, the coach, Bobby Kilpatrick, kept his promise and made Dave his starting shortstop. He would up having a fine year, hitting .395 and making all-Metro conference. The coach must have known something when he promised him the job.

"He must have made some phone calls about me," Dave feels. "There were many coaches in the area who had already told me to forget football and concentrate on baseball. The only problem there was all my scholarship offers were for football. But now I was playing at Memphis, so it didn't matter."

Dave played semi-pro ball in Memphis that summer, and when he returned to school in the fall of 1980, Coach Kilpatrick told him to forget football, that he would put him on a baseball scholarship.

"I figured if I went back for baseball I'd knock someone else out of a scholarship. They only had 13½ baseball scholarships available at one time, while they had 30 a year in football. Football had been providing me with everything until then, so I decided to stick it out. I was mainly a punter by then, and I felt I had a chance to do some kicking for the team that year, anyway."

He ended up the number two punter that fall, so he didn't play again. But then came baseball and all else was forgotten. The team was very good that year, 1981, winding up 48-11 and going to the eastern regional playoffs where they lost to a fine South Carolina team, which went on to the Final Four. But Dave and his teammates broke a slew of records that year.

"I think I broke 12 or 13 school marks," Dave recalls.

"I hit .396 with 14 home runs and 61 RBI's. I also had 87 hits and stole 39 bases in 41 tries. My career batting average for two years was .395 with 22 home runs, both records. I also had a total of 145 hits and 55 of 58 stolen bases. I also had the record for assists and runs scored, season and career, and the records for total bases and double plays, among others."

Naturally, with that kind of play Dave was attracting the attention of plenty of pro scouts, especially his second year when he seemed to be constantly talking to someone. He had been pointing toward a pro career since he was in high school.

"It was kind of funny," he says, "I knew I wanted baseball and really did everything in baseball, but football paid for it. Football gave me room, board, food, anything I wanted. In baseball, half the guys were on partials and had to pay for their books and tuition, some living at home. They had it tough."

But he was now eligible for the draft and the wheels began turning. Fortunately, his coach was able to help him, since he himself had once played in the White Sox organization and pretty much knew what Dave was going through. It really started to get heavy when Memphis State went down to the Metro tournament that year. That's when Dave met Carl Lowenstein of the Dodgers, who had seen him play a terrible game earlier in the year against Tennessee. But they were still interested and along with some other teams were asking him if he would sign if he was drafted. Dave said, sure. He was ready.

"I probably played the best ball of my life in that tournament," he recalls. "Everything was going good, the swing was there, I was making good plays in the field. Even though we eventually lost, I hit .632, and that couldn't have hurt me. When I returned to school everyone was telling me that I'd be drafted. The question was, how high? When the school year ended I couldn't decide whether to go home to Florida or not. I didn't know whether I should start working because I didn't want to start a job and then get drafted and have to leave it in a week. So I waited."

There were more calls from scouts. This time they were trying to find out how much Dave would want to sign.

"You tell them draft me and we'll find out," Dave quipped. "You don't want to give yourself away like that. The day of the draft I was sure someone would take me, but I still didn't know how high. I was thinking that I still had two more years of baseball eligibility left. I had a minor in accounting at Memphis State and if I returned to school I was going to make it my major. So I did have a choice.

"I was really tense the day of the draft. I was up early and the time just seemed to drag. By noon I hadn't heard and couldn't take it any longer, so I called the school. They told me they thought it was just starting. By then the phone was ringing off the hook as all my friends and relatives were calling to see if I'd been drafted. And every time it rang I was jumping a mile. Then I'd have to hustle them off so I could try to keep the line open.

"About 30 minutes later I got the call. I knew I must have gone early to get a call so soon. It was Carl Lowenstein and he told me the Dodgers had taken me on the first round. That had to be one of the most exciting moments of my entire life. I practically jumped through the roof. Carl kept talking and I just wanted to get him off the phone so I could tell everybody."

That night Dave couldn't sleep, wondering what would happen the next day when the Dodgers came in with an offer. The next night Carl Lowenstein came over and they began talking. Dave's parents were still in Florida, so Bobby Kilpatrick came over to help him out. He didn't sign that night because he wanted his parents there. The next night they all started arriving. His wife's mother came, then his parents.

"As the people came in I had to explain everything all over to them," Dave says, "so I didn't sign until four o'clock in the morning. Then we all went out and had breakfast. It was quite a couple of days."

The Dodgers were assigning Dave to their Class A team at Vero Beach, so he and Gina had to begin packing to return to Florida. They went to Dave's home in St. Petersburg and had a few parties to celebrate. The Florida State League played a split season, so he had to report very shortly. Then the day before he was set to report, there was a family crisis.

His wife's father suffered a serious stroke in Tallahassee, Florida. At first they didn't think he'd live through the night. So Dave had to go to Tallahassee with Gina and couldn't report. He stayed a day or so as his father-in-law remained in a coma. Finally, there was nothing he could do, so he left his wife behind and reported to Vero Beach. His father would stay in the coma for some six weeks before he began to recover, so Gina was going back and forth, and the added pressure of his illness and his wife's grief stayed with Dave as he began his professional career.

The first big adjustment Dave had was converting to a wooden bat. He had been using aluminum through college.

"All of the college teams I saw used aluminum," he said. "You have a choice, but with an aluminum bat the ball jumps so much better. If they used them in the big leagues you'd have infielders and pitchers getting killed and there would be guys hitting 75 or 80 home runs a year.

"The aluminum bat is lighter, so with it you can have bad fundamentals and bad everything, yet still get the head of the bat out, which is the big part of hitting. You can get jammed with a pitch and still get a basehit. With a wood bat you've got to get the head out or you don't get a thing. So I had to struggle awhile before I could get the head of the bat out. But most players going from college to pro ball have to make that adjustment. I'd say it took me a good two weeks to get used to the wood."

Dave said there isn't that much time for any intensive instruction when you first arrive, because the season is starting and there are games every day. You just take batting practice and play. The real teaching comes in the Instructional League when the instructors and coaches can really study what you're doing.

It was tough for Dave at the beginning. His teammates would ride him about being the number one choice, and he even heard it from the fans. So expectations were high and he began putting pressure on himself, which didn't help his play.

"I can remember saying to myself many times, Hey, I'm the number one pick and I've got to do something. That didn't make it any easier. I began trying to do things I couldn't do yet. I made stupid plays and I wasn't thinking."

Dave tried to get help with his hitting from people like his old high school coach and even his father. They knew him from the past and were in a better position to see what he was doing wrong, he felt.

"The Dodger people hadn't known me that long, so they really hadn't seen me when I was hitting well. It's funny, but even my mom knew it wasn't me at the plate. And my old high school coach told me I was pressing, that I wasn't relaxing. My coaches at Vero tried to keep my spirits up and threw me all the batting practice I wanted. It took about two months when I started to come out of it. I was hitting .206 at the time and I thought they were gonna fire my scout for signing me."

Though Dave didn't realize it at the time, his family problems were also affecting his play. When he was at his lowest point with the .206 average, his father-in-law was just beginning to really improve from his stroke. Up to then, it had been extremely hard on Dave's wife and he was trying to get up there to see them every chance he had.

"I remember talking to a guy I had worked with in Florida who had done some coaching for the Minnesota Twins," said Dave. He began telling me how he had talked to some great players over the years, guys like Reggie Jackson, Jim Rice, and Rod Carew. He said one of the most important things they all had in common was the ability to wipe everything else out of their minds and concentrate on what they were doing, especially when they came up to hit. You have to go to the plate with your eye on nothing but the ball. Any kind of distraction will mess you up.

"When I thought about that I said, hey, that's me! I was going up to the plate with so many things on my mind and not concentrating on my hitting. I was thinking about my wife, my father-in-law, the fans, my teammates, how I looked, and what people were going to think of me. I even let the crowd get to me, something I hadn't done in my entire life. But, then again, I had never been booed before in my life, either."

Dave sums up his problems by twisting around an old cliche. "Most people have problems taking their work home," he says. "I was having problems because I was taking my home to work."

The last part of the season things went much smoother. Gina's father was on the road to recovery and Dave began playing the kind of ball expected from a top choice. He ended the 1981 campaign with a respectable .270 batting average in 65 games. He had eight doubles, a triple, and 18 runs batted in. His good eye enabled him to draw 49 walks, and he stole 15 bases.

"I learned that wherever you go, you've got to prove yourself all over again, from Little League on up," he said. "I have proved it time and again in the past, but still, when you get to the pros you're nothing. So I'm the number one pick. Big deal. Number 25 is the same guy. You've got to start from scratch. I think that all got to me. But over the course of the season I learned to wipe that out and just play the game."

After the season ended Dave went to Arizona for Instructional ball, and that's when he says the Dodgers really started working with him. He learned more about the game there than he ever had in his life.

"We'd start at 9:30 in the morning and just work on the different skills, like cut-offs one day, double plays another, pickoffs a third day, and everything the way they do it throughout the Dodger system, right up to the big club. They work on everything—catching, throwing, sliding, hitting, running. You would think that having played the game since I was eight years old I would know how to run the bases. Well, I didn't.

"For one thing I was lunging to first bases instead of running through the bag. Then there was one game when I took too wide a turn around second and was thrown out at third by a step. Afterward, one of the coaches told me I had taken two extra steps because of my turn. If I had cut the bag properly, I would have been safe. So we worked on all kinds of little things like that."

Dave estimates that Instructional ball helped him to improve some 50 to 75 percent. Now he's waiting to see where he will play in 1982. He doesn't feel he proved much in his first season, but he's still hoping to play Double A. But if he's returned to A ball for another year, no problem. He figures he's got time, though his goal remains very constant.

"When you're young and dreaming about playing professionally," he says, "you think just starting in the minors would be great. But when you get there, you realize that in A ball you're nothing. Many people have told me that I've accomplished a lot. I've made it to the pros. But I won't feel I've accomplished anything until I reach the big leagues. I just won't feel gratified until I get there."

That kind of sums it up for minor league ballplayers everywhere. It's great to be drafted and sign. It's fine to be playing in the minors, learning and making friends. But it isn't over until you get there, to the major leagues. The odds aren't good, but all minor leaguers feel they'll make it, or they wouldn't be playing in the first place. That's certainly the way Dave Anderson feels and will continue to feel as he strives to become one of the baseball stars of tomorrow.

THE MANAGERS

One of the most vital positions within a minor league organization is that of manager. These are the men most responsible for molding future major leaguers, and it's a multi-dimensional job, a lot more than filling out a lineup card and changing pitchers. Among other things, a minor league manager must be a teacher, a disciplinarian, a friend, a father figure, a tactician, a psychologist, a coach, a role model, a motivator, a diplomat, and a shrewd judge of baseball talent.

And there was a time not so many years ago when he also had to be a groundskeeper, a batting practice pitcher, an equipment man, and even a bus driver. That because in the past the minor league manager was a one-man show. He had to handle everything by himself. He didn't have the fulltime coaches and roving instructors to help him out. Thank goodness for small things.

The success of the Dodger organization has to be credited to all the personnel, and that includes the fine men managing the various minor league teams. Two of the best are Stan Wasiak and Del Crandall. Though they operate at different ends of the minor league chain, and have varied baseball backgrounds, the results have been the same. Both do a first class job.

Stan Wasiak is a real veteran and a class guy. He's a former minor league player who might have made it to the Bigs had he not spent four of his peak playing years in the armed forces during World War II. Shortly afterward he began his minor league managing career, and now has the record for most consecutive years skippering in the minors. The 1982 season will mark his 33rd straight season as a pilot. He currently handles the Dodgers Class A club at Vero Beach.

Del Crandall, on the other hand, is a former All-Star catcher with the Milwaukee Braves. He was the man behind the mask when the Braves won the World Series in 1957 and again when they were beaten the following year. He became a manager shortly after his playing days ended, has managed in the minors, coached in the majors, then piloted the Milwaukee Brewers of the American League from 1972 to 1975. He has been managing the Dodgers Triple A club at Albuquerque since 1978, and has won the last two Pacific Coast League championships.

Let's take a closer look at these two men and the way they go about their demanding jobs.

The Chicago Cubs drafted Stan Wasiak out of high school in 1940. He then had pretty much of a nomadic minor league existence until 1950, when the Dodgers' resident genius, Branch Rickey, tabbed him as managerial timber.

"I was 30 years old and still playing in the minors," Stan recalls. "One day I was sitting in a restaurant talking with another ballplayer and Mr. Rickey was sitting across from us. We were talking baseball and he must have overheard us. He liked the way I played anyway, a lot of drive and hustle, and he told me he'd like me to be a manager in the Dodger organization. He offered me something like $4,000 a year and for the next eight years

BASEBALL STARS OF TOMORROW

I was a playing manager. I played with and managed many of the old Brooklyn Dodgers before leaving the organization in 1954, though I continued as a playing manager with Detroit's minor league clubs. I later joined the White Sox organization for a few years and in 1969 rejoined the Dodgers."

Stan has managed at every level, from Triple A on down, but says he is happiest working with kids at the A level.

"At the A level I find I can try to make professionals out of the kids quickly. The quicker I can do that the more I'm doing for the organization, Stan explained. "At that level I can still scare the kids a little bit and I don't have to deal with a bunch of agents, which the kids already have when they get to Double and Triple A.

"I get a tremendous amount of satisfaction from the job. At the organizational meetings, scouts often tell me that they love to send the kids to me, that I can work 'em good and know how to develop ballplayers. We all like to feel important and get an occasional pat on the back. I'm doing what I feel I do best in life. Manage.

"The big thing I've found you need at this level is patience. You get that from experience. Many organizations try to get off cheap at the Class A level and hire a young kid to manage. So you've got a kid of 26 or 27, who has played maybe Triple A ball, now managing kids 18 and 19. It's not hard to ruin a kid of that age if you don't handle him carefully. That's why I say there are too many real experienced managers at the A level."

Stan admits that there was a time he wanted to manage in the Bigs, but the opportunity never came. Now, he just wants to remain where he is. His home is in Mobile, Alabama, and Vero Beach is just 600 miles away. He would like to stay at Vero until he retires.

Things are much better for a minor league manager

today at every level. Stan recalls the many years he worked alone, when he was the jack-of-all-trades, including trainer and bus driver. Plus the busses then weren't air-conditioned, didn't have toilet facilities or reclining seats. In addition, the ballparks were bad back then. Many didn't have clubhouses and as Stan says, if you had a nail in the wall you had a good locker.

"The owners finally realized they just couldn't get so much from one man, that three heads were better than one. You can't watch 25 some odd guys by yourself and give them all a fair shake. So now I have two fulltime coaches in addition to the roving instructors.

There has also been a subtle change in the players coming into the minors today as opposed to years ago. For openers, Stan says the players in the old days were hungrier, more determined to make it. Many kids today outsmart themselves, he says. They often think they're much better than they are and they don't bear down.

"The kids today are better educated on the whole," he continued. "More kids came straight out of high school when I played and not even that sometimes during the Depression. Kids today are also better trained when they sign. They have better instructors at all levels. They also have alternatives. In many cases a kid can make more money on the outside than he can in the low minors. In my time we didn't have a job to go back home to. You were forced to bust your fanny to try to make it in pro ball.

"Pride was a real big thing to us, and I sometimes wonder how much pride the kids today have. I find a little different attitude now than I did before. Of course, the real good ones still have pride. And if I don't see it I'll try to get down on the kid real quick. I stress how important pride is, and being a Dodger, also."

Stan then explained why a good Class A manager has

to be a disciplinarian and often a father figure.

"I try to make them professionals, both on and off the field. Once they put on that uniform and the game starts it's all business with me. I've been in the game too long not to realize that once you or your coaches begin to let down a little, the club will quit on you very quickly. The kids just won't play well; they'll think it's a big joke. So you've got to have discipline and instill in them the importance of baseball as a team game."

A young player coming into Class A can run into a number of problems that don't usually occur once he makes it to Double and Triple A. For one thing, Stan explained, most of the kids coming into the minors have been outstanding players all their lives, from Little League right up through high school and college. They come in with a nice bonus and have that nice big ego going for them.

"Suddenly, they're in professional baseball and they meet their equals," Stan explained. "They're no longer the big stars. And if they start out poorly they often get down on themselves and then they're in real trouble right away. This is the time you've really got to bolster them up. You say, listen, you're my second baseman, shortstop or whatever. Don't worry about it and don't press."

Stan also finds many of his first year players getting homesick, especially when they're not going well. He says it can happen more so in some of the smaller towns, where a kid feels lonely and isolated. He recalls one kid this past season from a small town in North Carolina. Stan says he was a quiet kid and you just knew he was really homesick. Stan talked to him very often and kidded with him whenever he had the chance.

"That's the way I communicate with them," he said. "I kid with them, get them in the office and ask them about their families, try to loosen them up a bit. I'll tell them how important they are to the ballclub and try to make the boy want to stay. Our general manager at Vero, Terry Reynolds, also does an outstanding job with the kids. We often have little outings for everyone after the day games, and that kind of brings us all together."

The qualities that Stan looks for in his young players are basically the same as the Dodger scouts seek. So hopefully by the time the players are delivered to him, they're ready to have their natural skills honed.

"Back when he was starting this Dodger organization, Mr. Rickey said he believed in two things, which he called God's gift," Stan said. "That's the arm and the legs. We can't teach a kid to run faster or throw harder. Attitude means a great deal, as does the aptitude for learning the fine points of the game. But usually when a kid has the arm and the legs, then we can do something.

"Speed is so essential, both offensively and defensively. One reason the Oakland team did so well last year was those three jackrabbits Billy Martin had in the outfield—Henderson, Murphy, and Armas. Those guys hauled down balls all year that would have been doubles and triples with other outfields. And that kind of stuff doesn't appear in the papers. It's definitely a faster game now than it was, say, 15 years ago. Look how stealing the bases has come back.

"I like a ballclub that can run. I'm the type of manager who likes to use the speed to steal, bunt, hit and run. It's more exciting baseball. The fans love it more, too. They want to see the kids running and running. And in the low minors we can do those kinds of things without being second-guessed by sportswriters and media people. Our job is to develop talents. It's nice to win, but it's not paramount."

One of the most gratifying parts of Stan Wasiak's job

is to watch a kid he's developed and matured. He was the manager at Lodi in 1979 when Fernando Valenzuela pitched his first professional game. "He didn't have that scroogie," Stan said, "but he had an outstanding curve and was sneaky fast, though not overpowering the way you like to see. But he learned the scroogie in a hurry and with his control was on his way."

The veteran manager also got a thrill last year when the Dodgers brought up young Steve Sax from San Antonio to replace the injured Davey Lopes at second base.

"I had Steve two years ago and then last year he was in the World Series," Stan recalled. "When I got him he was a kid without a set position, and we made a second baseman out of him. He then had a heck of a year at San Antonio, hitting, fielding, hustling all over the place like Pete Rose. Then look at the job he did when he was called up. That's really the way to develop them.

"I saw him play last year when the Dodgers were playing Houston one night. After the game Steve came up to me and said, 'Stan, if it wasn't for you I wouldn't be here.' That really made me happy and makes my job worthwhile. You know, Vero Beach isn't New York or Chicago or Los Angeles. You don't get much ink. So when someone thanks you personally, like Steve Sax did, it really makes you feel good."

One of the hardest parts of Stan's or any manager's job is dealing with the kid who isn't going to make it, and has to be released.

"Yeah, it's tough," Stan acknowledges. "In most cases the kid kind of senses it. He knows. But you try to play him now and then, and try to help him. Slowly, you try to talk to him a bit, try to explain things to him. But as I say, deep inside he knows it's a matter of time. And it always seems to be the nice kid, the good kid, the kid who never causes you any trouble. Of course, if you had a kid who couldn't play too well and was a wiseguy to boot, you would get rid of him as soon as you could. But it's the toughest part of the job. They're nice kids and they're deeply hurt, no question about it.

"I've seen so many cases. Some kids cry, others get mad at you. But the way I feel about it is that I'm doing them a favor because the kid is not going to make it in this profession. He's got his whole life in front of him and it's not the end of the world. Everybody can't be a big league ballplayer and I try to explain this to them. And I tell them if they think I'm wrong to go somewhere and prove I'm wrong. They don't have to quit. But if you don't think a kid is major league caliber, you have to be honest with him."

Stan said that some kids bounce around the minors. They hook up with another organization at the same classification, maybe even go up one more notch. But as Stan says, the Dodgers don't release kids unless they know they're not prospects, and it's a consensus of opinion, not just a single manager or scout. If a kid can't play, there's no sense wasting time and space, or as Stan says spinning our wheels.

There are other ways in which Stan goes easy on his kids. He doesn't have a dress code at Vero Beach, explaining that the kids might as well be comfortable when riding the bus to a small town. Plus it's very hot in Florida and he'd rather keep the kids relaxed. The thing that does drive him nuts are the tape machines and radios that so many youngsters have nowadays. Sometimes it gets so loud he practically begs them to get earphones.

But on the whole, Stan Wasiak finds it easier to handle the kids at the A level. The attitude at Triple A, for instance, is often much different.

"At Triple A, a lot of guys think you can't teach them anymore," he says. "There are always guys who are mad

BASEBALL STARS OF TOMORROW

because they aren't in the majors and guys who are sore because they have been sent down from the big club. And then you've got the general manager of the big club calling you all the time to find out who's doing well, and you've got more sportswriters looking for stories and second guessing you. All these little things and more emphasis on winning, winning, winning.

"Don't get me wrong. I love to win and hate to lose. But if you do lose in Class A, you're still developing kids. You always have to win in Triple A and in the big leagues. And there's simply more teaching in A ball. At Triple A, they had better know the fundamentals."

Stan said that fundamentals are constantly stressed in A ball, as well as the elimination of mental errors. He hates to send a kid up to the next level and find out he's making mistakes on the basepaths, or failing to be aware of the number of outs, or throwing to the wrong base, things like that.

Obviously, Stan Wasiak is a man who takes his job seriously. Could it be any other way with a man who has managed for more than 30 consecutive years and has won more than 2,000 games? He must be doing something right. He's also dedicated to helping the youngsters, the kids who are just starting out. It's just as important to have a solid man at the Class A level as it is in the Bigs. And as Stan Wasiak himself has said, it's what he does best. The record speaks for itself.

For Del Crandall, the task is both different and the same. For instance, like Stan Wasiak his primary job is developing players for the big club. And like his Class A counterpart, Del Crandall has only recently received the help of two fulltime coaches. He, too, ran a one-man show before that, doing all the jobs from soup to nuts.

Unlike Wasiak, Del Crandall is dealing with older

players, men more than boys in many cases, and players who should have a solid foundation in the fundamentals before they reach Triple A. He admits, though, that all players don't leave their problems at A and Double A ball; they sometimes bring them right along. He's also involved in moving players at a very sensitive time. Players at Albuquerque are just a step away from the majors. Many of them think they already belong, so Del has to try to keep the delicate balance between the players' egos and their abilities.

He must be doing his job well, because he has had to handle some tough problems of players going up and down, and yet his Albuquerque Dukes have won a pair of PCL titles in 1980 and 1981, this past year roaring through the Coast League like one of General Patton's juggernauts. And the camaraderie on his club, enhanced greatly by their on-field success, helped ease some of the players' gripes and discontents.

Del, of course, has managed in both the majors and the minors, and says the basic difference is the overall philosophy.

"In the minor leagues you're developing players," he says. "In the big leagues you're expected to win. Not that they don't like you to win in the minors. They do. But player development and feeding the major league club is the primary objective. If you lose a key player or two to the big club during the heat of your own pennant race, you can't complain, because your first loyalty is to the organization."

Del says that the great reduction in the number of minor leagues and number of teams within each organization has also somewhat altered the overall minor league philosophy.

"In the days when you had 55 or so leagues, there were so many players within the organization that the tendency was to let them play and figure the cream would come to the top," he explained. "It isn't that way now. You still have to rely on talent, of course, but there are so few players that you concentrate more on trying to develop that talent more quickly than they did years ago. They used to let you play yourself into the big leagues. Now they attempt to instruct you into the big leagues."

There were good players, according to Del, who didn't reach the majors in years past until they were 28 or 29 years old. Today a guy like Jack Perconte is beginning to worry that his age may be held against him, and he's just 27. So the rush to get players ready also puts more pressure on the manager.

Del also mentioned a special kind of minor leaguer he calls an organizational player. That's a guy who, because of his makeup, is looked upon as a possible future manager or coach. This type of player is often kept in the organization longer than his playing talent would ordinarily dictate. He's also useful sometimes in filling roster spots to make sure each team in the organization remains competitive.

Like Stan Wasiak, Del Crandall sees today's player as very different from the players of the past.

"They have to be different to a certain degree because they are products of the society that now exists," Del says. "People in all professions are different, but that doesn't mean they aren't as dedicated or don't love the game as much as anybody did. The game still means a great deal to them.

"But you have to approach them a little differently. For instance, in my day we were more used to taking orders. When someone in authority told you to do something you'd say, yes sir. You would do your best to please. Now you have to deal with the questions, with the doubts that what you're saying is the right thing. They say things like, my Little League coach said to do it this way or my college coach said to do it that way. So you have to consistently convince these people that what you're saying has merit. So no matter where you are managing it's a matter of your players having confidence in you."

Because his players know he is a former major league star, they tend to respect him more readily than otherwise. But Del says it won't last long if he doesn't keep earning it over and over again.

"Being a former player can work for just so long," he admits. "Certainly if a Sandy Koufax comes in to talk to our kids they're going to listen right away. But if he were to become someone they couldn't listen to, then all his fame would quickly go by the wayside. It wouldn't matter. Sandy, of course, is an outstanding individual who does keep your interest and your confidence."

Once a manager has the confidence of his players he can operate on several levels. Naturally, he's working to develop their ballplaying talents. But he's also in a better position to help the kids with any personal problems they might have.

"I don't mean I can solve every problem," Del says, "but I try to get a kid to understand that everybody has problems, and he's got to be able to deal with them so he can mentally be ready to play ball to the best of his ability.

"We have a 22-man roster at Albuquerque and of those 22 players you may have just four or five who really need a lot of attention. In fact, those four or five will probably take up most of your time. It's not really baseball instruction, but it overlaps. For example, if you have a player who doesn't know how to live right, it will show up at the ballpark. Or if you have somebody whose family is getting him down, it will show up at the ballpark. I guess the bottom line is whatever you can do to help a kid get the most out of his ability, well, that's what has to be done."

While not going as far as to call himself a father figure, Del admits the players do need somebody to talk to and confide in, someone they feel is not going to put them down. "I don't know how other managers approach it, but as far as I'm concerned that's part of my relationship with the players I have."

Though Del himself doesn't bar a return to the major league managerial ranks sometime in the future, there's a kind of purity of spirit among the players that he really enjoys.

"You still have players striving in the minor leagues without any of those outside things to spoil them," he says. "This is not an indictment of big leaguers, because there are some super people up there. But in the minors they're still striving and I think that can affect their approach to the game, their openness, and how receptive they are."

Just as Stan Wasiak spoke about attitude and mental aptitude, Del Crandall talks of players having the right makeup to fully utilize their talents. They have to have a mental toughness and the ability to adjust to situations. That's the only way they'll make progress, Del says. These adjustments must be made at each level.

"Unfortunately, you probably find the guys with the best attitude are the ones who don't have the super ability," said Del. "I guess that's because the better players have been told how good they are ever since they were in Little League. As a consequence, they become very, very resistant to change or suggestion. They feel their ability is going to take them all the way, like everyone has been telling them for so long."

In some ways, Del keeps a tighter rein on his players in Triple A than Stan Wasiak does at A ball. But, again, there's a different situation. Del's players are almost to the majors.

"I have a dress code of sorts," he says. "No ties, but jackets when we travel and also when we come to the ballpark. I don't like T-shirts and cutoffs and tennis shoes. I'm a little more relaxed at home, but on the road we try to dress as though we're proud of what we do.

"I also have rules for curfews and times to be at the park. I haven't checked on players for a long time, but I still have the curfew in case someone decides he wants to be out and I happen to see him. Then he's subject to a fine. But I don't try to be a policeman with them. They have to live their own lives and have to learn to discipline themselves as far as their free time is concerned. At the same time if I happen to see them or I know somebody is starting to do some things that aren't going to help him or the club, then I try to do whatever I can."

Del was also very open and candid when discussing the racial situation in the minors today, or at least how he perceives it to be. First of all, he feels the racial thing between players doesn't really exist anymore. "I just haven't seen anything to suggest it does," he said. But he also talked about the situation in terms of the manager.

"I believe that a white manager must be careful about how he handles himself around Latin players and some black players. Some of them have a tendency to put things on a racial basis," he explained. "I can only speak for myself. You feel you treat everyone the same, but it's the interpretation. You try to understand to the best of your ability where people come from and what their backgrounds are and what problems they might bring with them because of that. But there are very, very few problems anymore. I think there were more years ago."

He also said there is some language problems with Latin players, especially if the player is a pitcher or a catcher. Then, Del said, it's very difficult because there's so much that goes on in that area. Being an ex-catcher Del gets involved more deeply with his batteries and often finds he is limited in how much he can contribute where the language factor is involved.

Another area that often has to be handled delicately is the moving of players. For one thing, once a player reaches Triple A there is very little chance of him ever going back to Double A. It's kind of make or break by then. Del says that player moves are usually handled by Bill Schweppe and himself, with Dodger general manager Al Campanis also getting involved. In fact, Del said that Bill Schweppe often initiates the moves because he follows the players very carefully and often knows more about the needs of the other clubs than Del does. He might suggest to Del that one of his players be returned to Double A so he can play every day. Al Campanis usually comes into it when the player is on a major league contract and they are considering bringing him up to the parent club. When Del needs a player to replace one who has moved up, that's handled by Bill Schweppe and the Double A manager involved.

One of the toughest problems is dealing with a player who is being demoted or released. Del agrees with Stan Wasiak in feeling that the player usually knows it's coming.

"I'm still the one who has to tell him," he says. "And even though they know it's coming, they usually don't want to admit it. But probably the biggest problem is when a player comes back from the big leagues and feels he should have stayed there. I usually try to give him a lot of room and let him sort of hang himself before I get into it. It takes some of them a week or two to adjust, and then they play their way through it.

"But they come back with a terrible attitude most of the time. They're disappointed for openers, and they have gotten used to the convenience of the majors—the travel, the meal money, the cities, the hotels. All of these things have a bearing on their outlook, not just wearing the big league uniform. And it hurts to be no longer called a big leaguer. All these things affect them when they come back down."

The manager at the Triple A level must also deal with players looking for a way to reach the majors and ask to change positions or for a trade. Sometimes they will ask Del to please help them get out of the organization because they don't feel they'll make the majors as a Dodger. Del passes these requests along to Bill Schweppe. There is more of this today than years ago when players were more content to wait their turn. The money probably has something to do with it, and the impatience of the entire society at all levels.

Then there is the player who feels he isn't getting a fair shake and begins griping, perhaps threatening to cause dissension on the ballclub. This, too, has to be dealt with by the manager.

"Well, you hope it never reaches that stage," Del said, "because if it does you really haven't been paying any attention to what has been going on. You have to try to deal with those things as quickly as you can without giving a player an opportunity to solve the problem himself. Ideally, the best way would be to allow him to solve it himself, but you can't let it go on too long where it might become a way of life with him.

"So when you talk to him you've got to try to have enough ammunition, better arguments, because you're dealing with intelligent people and they can usually understand when they're being unreasonable. You can usually do this successfully if you've taken the time to develop the right relationship with the player in the first place."

It all sounds pretty complex, and it is. No wonder Del says the biggest addition to the minor league club has been the two fulltime coaches. He has so many other things to think about that someone has to help in the instruction, and interestingly enough, he feels that baseball needs more developing than the other major sports.

"Basketball has size, which is dominating," he says. "Football has strength, which is dominating. All sports need mental toughness, no matter what. You've got to have that mental aspect of the game. But take football, for instance. You've got a guy with toughness who weighs 260 pounds. He's been through high school and college as a defensive tackle and he can control the guy across the line from him. From there, the X's and O's permit him to play the game, and things are pretty much cut and dried.

"But baseball isn't that type of game. It's a game of reaction, a game where you have to develop all the offensive and defensive skills. And trying to hit a baseball is one of the toughest things to do in all sports."

So the manager has his work cut out for him. Besides all the things Stan Wasiak and Del Crandall talked about, there are daily reports that must be filed, meetings with scouts, with other managers, and with Bill Schweppe. It's a demanding, fulltime job that only a real professional can do successfully. You're dealing with skills and talents that must be developed, and individual personalities that must be fully understood. For the manager is not developing a pitcher, or a first baseman, or a centerfielder. He's developing a whole person, physical skills and mental outlook, to produce that rare breed known as a major league baseball player.

LIFE IN THE MINOR LEAGUES

What is it really like for a player to spend several years in baseball's minor leagues? What does he do in his spare time; what does he talk about; what concerns him the most about his future? He comes to the minors from high school or college, and he must make adjustments. He must learn to prepare himself to play baseball almost every day. He must become a constant traveler. He must make friends with and live with a variety of people from all parts of the country. He must learn to live right, to eat and sleep and take care of his body while staying in a variety of hotels and motels. He must often leave his wife and family behind.

Let's face it. This is not your ordinary, everyday, nine to five lifestyle. And the minor leagues are not really big time, though the consensus is that things are much better now than they were in years past. That includes just about everything—the ballparks, the motels, the mode of travel. But it still isn't easy, especially when you add the pressure of trying to advance and make it to the Bigs.

In the old days when there were more teams and more independent owners, there were often more crazy kinds of promotions, more of a circus type atmosphere, though that hasn't disappeared altogether. In fact, there is even more of a carnival atmosphere at many major league parks today, with promotions designed to bring fans through the turnstyles. Sometimes the more things change the more they stay the same.

Stan Wasiak has been around minor league life the longest, and he related a pair of incidents coming some 40 years apart, that show the minors always have that occasional whacky quality.

"This one is hard to believe," Stan relates, "but in 1941 when I was playing in Grand Rapids, Michigan, there was this Hindu fellow who they buried behind home plate in a box with no tubes for air or nothing. Then we went out and played the game, and when it was over they dug him up. He was under there the entire game.

"Sure, it was a publicity stunt. He got about a hundred bucks for it and he was a little groggy when he came out. Later, he told us he had enough air in there for about two and a half to three hours. He used to do it to make money. One time he said he got scared because water was seeping into the box. I wouldn't do that for a billion dollars, I mean, the guy was buried right behind the plate umpire the whole time we were playing."

Stan also related some other stories from the old days, with guys jumping over cars, and an annual field day when one club would compete against another in crazy stunts. For instance they would tie about six guys' shoes together and put them out by second base. The guys would run out, find their shoes, untie them, and race back to home plate. They also had blindfolded wheelbarrow races with guys trying to find second base.

"It still happens," Stan continued. "Just last year or the year before we got a call from a guy named Boom

BASEBALL STARS OF TOMORROW

Boom Costa, something like that. He said he would blow himself up with dynamite around second base. Sure enough, he did his act at Vero Beach five straight days. Before the game he got in a box with a football helmet on and it really blew up. Crazy. And I remember a promotion back in 1977 or '78. I had an outfielder named Marv Garrison. He and Ricky Henderson, who's now with the A's, raced a horse a hundred yards. The horse won.

"So these things still happen in the minors. Last year we had a grocery contest. Contestants got to keep all the groceries they could put in a basket at first base, second and third in a set amount of time. It makes it fun for the fans, and the players get a kick out of it, too."

Comic relief never hurts, especially when there are some pretty rough things the players must adjust to. Perhaps the travel is the most legendary. The minors were always notorious for long bus rides and a rather rugged schedule. As mentioned earlier, the busses today are much better, and some of the leagues fly all or part of the time. But the long busrides still exist, and the players must adjust to the travel and grueling schedule in their own ways.

"Before I came into the minors I heard all about the terrible bus rides and playing almost every day, then riding the bus again all night," Jack Perconte recalls. "Everybody thought about it. But I found that those things don't really bother you because you just want to play. Having to play every day takes more getting used to than the travel."

Dave Stewart remembers bus rides in rookie ball that lasted up to 18 hours, but he liked the travel because they had fun. It was kid stuff, like pillow fights, hot foots, that kind of horsing around. But it was still tiring. Ricky Wright started off in Double A and didn't have as many bus trips. But he missed the home cooking from Texas, adding that he couldn't walk into too many places on the road and find good beans and cornbread.

Brian Williams agreed with Stewart, that travel in rookie league was very tiring, and it took its toll on his playing after awhile, but he had no complaints about the accommodations, the places the team stayed. Ted Power's reaction to road trips and travel was slightly different. Being one of the married players, he finds missing his wife and baby the hardest part of traveling, and admits there have been times when it has affected his play.

So on the whole the travel seems to be something all ballplayers quickly learn to tolerate. The bus rides in the low minors are a necessary evil, but you can find ways to enjoy them, even though they are tiring and often somewhat debilitating.

Of course, almost all young players hear about the travel before they sign. But everyone goes in with his own expectations of what the minors are going to be like. Sometimes things turn out quite differently, and other times they're just about as they were expected to be.

Dave Anderson's biggest surprise came the first time he walked into a minor league lockerroom.

"I was really surprised to see a lot of guys sitting there smoking cigarettes and others blasting their radios and having a good time. If anyone did that in college ball he would have been right back on the bus heading home. I found a much more relaxed atmosphere in the minors than in college. And I guess if you still do the job there's nothing wrong with it."

Ed Amelung found life in the minors much better than he thought it would be, and he credits the Dodger organization for that.

"We went to different camps during spring training and I could see the differences in their facilities compared with ours."

Ed also thought the players would all be great. "I expected all the pitchers were gonna throw 90 miles an hour and all the hitters were gonna hit rockets. Some guys were like that, of course, but not as many as I expected."

Ricky Wright says he knew about how things were going to be, and just wondered how he was going to handle things. He also expected to win more right away and had to adjust to taking his lumps. Brian Williams still expected to call the head man "coach" when he came in from high school. He learned very quickly that he now had a "manager," but it was OK to call him "skipper."

Ted Power expected more of a gung-ho attitude among players in pro ball. "A few teams have had it," he says, "but I would say the majority of teams don't have that rah-rah kind of spirit and attitude. The Albuquerque team in 1981 had it though. We got along great and liked playing together. It's certainly a more pleasant atmosphere when it's like that.

For Dave Stewart, the big shock in coming to the minors was learning how few players would make it to the majors.

"My first manager at Bellingham, Bill Berrier, told us that only about six of the 26 players on the team would play in the big leagues somewhere," Dave recalls. "That surprised me. But he was right. In fact, only one of us from that club has made it. Me. So he really let us know what it was going to be like before we got into it."

There were other things the players had to learn for themselves once they hit the minors. As Ricky Wright already said, he missed the home cooking, and he wasn't the only one. Players in the minors get a certain amount of money for food each day. The "meal money" increases as a player moves up in class. So it's kind of up to each individual player to spend what he wants on whatever kind of food he wants. It's easy to start gobbling up the so-called junk food and soft drinks, and again, it's up to the individual to more or less take care of himself as he sees fit.

"You have to learn to eat right," Jack Perconte commented. "When you have a hectic travel and playing schedule, eating right and getting rest become more important. Too much fast food and soda pop can hurt. I learned to drink more fresh fruit juices, things like that.

"But the meal money in the low minors when I was there was so minimal that you had to eat fast foods. I remember it being something like $6.50 for the entire day. Now, at Albuquerque, it's $14 a day, which isn't a whole lot. But players are making more in Triple A, also, so you can afford to spend more on better foods."

That seemed to be the prevalent opinion. You're not going to get home cooking, but if you take some pains you can still manage to eat pretty well.

In spite of the hectic schedule, the players occasionally have some time off. What they do with that time often depends on where they are and what their lifestyles are like. For instance, there are certain things available in Albuquerque that might not be so appealing in Lethbridge.

"Fishing is a big thing with a lot of guys here," said Del Crandall, "and so is golf to a certain degree. There are also a lot of horses around. But I guess sunning and swimming are what the players do most. They spend a lot of time out by the pool. We have a rule that they have to be out of the sun by two in the afternoon when we play at night. Too much sun can have a draining effect on them."

BASEBALL STARS OF TOMORROW

Some of the younger players, in their first or second seasons, still haven't had much time to think about recreation. Dave Anderson, for example, had illness in the family and was occupied with his wife and father-in-law whenever he could get away. So his time was filled. Ed Amelung lived on the beach in Florida, so he spent time playing volleyball, going bodysurfing and swimming. Being from California anyway, those things just came naturally to him.

For Brian Williams, also in his first year, sightseeing held a real fascination. "I just find it interesting being out on my own at seventeen and seeing new places and people. So I did a lot of sightseeing and picture taking when I had some free time during our road trips. Doing that also seemed to make me a little less homesick."

Ricky Wright, the Texan, is somewhat of a loner. He likes the wide open spaces and will often give anything to just find a quiet place to hunt or fish, his two main hobbies back home. He also enjoys listening to country music and relaxing by strumming his guitar. And there are always players who may gather over a beer or two and discuss the game and their futures in it.

The married players, of course, spend their free time with their families. All of the players have shared the experience of meeting others and making friends with players from other parts of the country and with different lifestyles. For the most part the players have found this an interesting part of minor league life. Don Crow, for instance, says he loves swapping stories with his new teammates.

"It was really kind of fun learning about different parts of the country from different guys," he said. "I found it an interesting experience because there are so many parts of the country where I've never been. I've talked to guys from Texas, from the south, and the east. My road roommate for two years was from Massachusetts, the opposite end of the country from my home, and I really enjoyed learning about that area and the lifestyles there."

Dave Stewart found it very satisfying to meet new people every year. "I never played with the same club twice, so every year there was a somewhat different group of people and I enjoyed making friends with them and then keeping in touch. There were no problems anywhere down the line because when you're kids you're kids. It doesn't make any difference how old you are. You're young guys with a lot in common sharing the same things."

For Dave Anderson, the philosophy and his style is simple. "A ballplayer is a ballplayer," he said, "anywhere you go. No problem making friends. I did just what I've always done in new situations. I keep my mouth shut, don't pop off, and let the friendships evolve slowly. I made a lot of good friends in a year, a cross section of guys from California to New York, and I enjoyed that very much."

Brian Williams was another who found the experience an interesting one. "I find it easier to get along with different kinds of guys because you're interested in one another," he said. "For me, it was interesting meeting guys from different and diverse places like Georgia and Vermont."

Though the consensus was pretty much the same about meeting people, that it was a positive, interesting, and easy experience, two players did express a slightly different view. Ted Power said he soon found out that he wasn't going to please everybody he met.

"I've always grown up in a small town atmosphere and my wife keeps telling me I'm too trusting," he says. "She says I sometimes let people walk on me. But I'll trust somebody until they prove I can't. I certainly didn't change just so I could get along with everybody from different parts of the country. One funny thing was that after a couple of years in the minors I began to feel like a misplaced Californian, because I like their lifestyle.

"Yet on the whole I think I got along with pretty much everyone. I've enjoyed playing on those teams where there was a real feeling of unity, no matter where the players came from. You don't always have that, but it's a real good atmosphere when you do."

The other player who had an occasional problem was Ricky Wright, who was again very candid in discussing it.

"To be honest about it," Ricky said, "I don't think a lot of people understand my way of life, don't appreciate the things I appreciate. For instance, if I'm driving down the road and see a guy who's been hunting walking with a handful of birds, I'm gonna want to stop and talk to him, because that interests me. I also had a roommate who, when he found I had asked my father to bring one of my guns down, told me he didn't want a gun in the house. He had never shot one and he didn't want it around. This happened last year at Albuquerque.

"I'm not trying to be bad or sound like a nut, but guns have always been part of my life. I like to hunt, enjoy tinkering with them, and shooting them. It's just part of me and I really miss that kind of thing when I'm away. I also like soft country music, and many of my roommates like the hard rock. Well, that stuff gives me a headache. But a lot of them would ask me how I could listen to the old, soft whiney stuff.

"So I've always had different interests than my roommates. When we'd go to a new place, one of my roommates would always want to go right into town. I always want to go out of town. For instance, in Salt Lake City (Utah), my roommates wanted to go right uptown and see what's there. I wanted to go to the mountains. What was inside the town doesn't really give me a buzz at all."

A man of strong and definite interests, Ricky Wright didn't always find it easy interacting with other people. So there are both sides to the question. A kind of offshoot of that is the fact that players are often competing for jobs against their own friends, or at least acquaintances. It seems that every player in the minors is acutely aware of his own position within the organization, and which players are up ahead at each level.

"You're very much aware of other players within the organization," said Ted Power. "There's a report that comes out every two weeks and you can follow everyone that way. Plus you've got friends around and they keep you informed about who's doing what. And you want to know this so you can compare yourself to others. I find that it's something that really has to be done. For instance, if it comes down to an argument on why you weren't called up and another guy was, you'll have exactly what that other guy has been doing.

"I think it's all right to kind of compete with a teammate at the same position if it pushes both of you to do better. And the most important thing no matter how you think about it is winning. To do that, you've got to be friends with your teammates."

Comparisons are commonplace, according to Dave Stewart. "There's always somebody watching," he said. "My last year in Triple A there were a lot of guys saying I should be called up because I'm doing this and doing that. So guys not only have opinions on where they should be, but on where other guys should be, as well."

In fact, Dave Stewart had an opinion on one of his

former teammates, Jack Perconte, who had spent so many years in the minors.

"Jack is an excellent ballplayer who probably should have been in the big leagues a year or two ago," Dave said. "I've played with him and I've never seen anyone play harder than Jack, or work as hard to get the job done."

Young players like Ed Amelung and Dave Anderson both admit they are well aware of players at their positions ahead of them. Amelung just shook his head and said, "There's a lot of them. The organization is full of fine players. I watch the box scores and they all seem to be doing well."

Shortstop Anderson says he can tell you the names and stats of all the other shortstops. "You want to know what the guys in front of you are doing, so you look at everything," he said. "But it's often a pretty friendly competition. I got to be friends with a shortstop ahead of me, Ross Jones, and he helped me out a bit with my fielding, saw some things I was doing wrong and told me about it. And I've learned a few things by watching him."

As a young player, Ted Power learned a hard lesson about friendships and competition in the minors.

"When they sent me to Lodi my first year in 1976, I didn't have a place to stay," he said. "There was another pitcher there named Steve McNulty, and he said I could stay with him until I found an apartment. So I stayed with him and I ended up taking his job. He was released and I filled his spot in the rotation.

"At first I really felt bad about it. But soon I realized it wasn't my fault. It was more his fault because he didn't perform. Yet the fact that he had been so nice to me and then I took his job really bothered me for awhile. But that's just the nature of the game. No matter what else, you've got to keep producing."

Perhaps it was Ricky Wright who again summed it up the best when he said, simply and succinctly:

"I think every guy in baseball can tell you who's ahead of him."

So there are many adjustments to be made by young players and a clear knowledge of what's ahead as far as the competition within the organization. There is something else waiting up ahead, especially for those who make it to the majors. No one can claim he doesn't think about it or that somewhere along the line it isn't a factor. That is the huge amount of money being offered today at the major league level. The thought of a multi-year, multi-million dollar contract just waiting for a new star to come and claim it must be a tantalizing image.

Most players today need agents to negotiate their contracts, and surprisingly, many players in the minor leagues are already represented, especially when they get to Triple A. That's when life starts to get complicated, as far as the bucks are concerned. When it comes to this, everyone has an opinion.

"The money is very important, but only to a certain extent when you're in the minors," is the way Don Crow feels. "Nobody in his right mind can expect to go up to the big leagues and become a star. You can't plan on it. Sure, everyone knows the money is there, but I've never heard a player come out and say, 'I'm gonna go up there and make a million dollars.' That's just not the thing, especially at Triple A. The immediate goal is to get to the big leagues, and that's what everybody is concentrating on."

Jack Perconte first got an agent when he went on a major league contract after three years in the minors. He said it was an intimidating situation for him to have to negotiate with Al Campanis, so he decided to get some representation. In Jack's experience, the money wasn't talked about a whole lot, though he said it definitely comes into play.

"A lot of people look toward it," he said. "I guess you have to think about it because it's there. It's got to be a little incentive for some guys. But it's never—and I say this but I don't know how much I believe it—it's never been that big a thing for me, because I'd just like to get a chance to play. Then again, I'm sure I wouldn't throw the money away, either."

Jack also said that some minor leaguers feel the big leaguers are overpaid, though others feel if it's there, why not take it.

"Each person sort of justifies it in his own way," he said. "If I was making a million dollars, I might have difficulty justifying it. I do think that some of the players are overpaid, but that's the way our system is. You get what you can."

From what Ricky Wright has seen, the money is a dream of a lot of players.

"I can't lie," he said, "if a guy came up and offered me a million dollars a year I don't think I'd have too many worries about too many things. I'd still want to go out and continue to win baseball games, but my gosh, that would take a lot of pressure off your mind right there. I personally don't think there's a player in baseball worth a million dollars, but then again, if a man offers it to you it's hard not to accept."

Both Dave Stewart and Ted Power agreed that it's more important to worry about getting to the majors than about the money you might make once you're there.

"After I put my time in and prove I can win, then I'd like to make lots of money," said Ted Power. "I've had a long enough road already so I know I'm going to have to pay my dues before I make those big bucks. But I guess everybody thinks about that pot of gold, having that one big year and cashing in. Realistically, though, if you think about it too much it can be like hitting your head against a brick wall. Pretty soon you won't concentrate on your job, and if you end up failing it will be your own fault."

Then there are the young players. Before he was even drafted, Dave Anderson received a big shock.

"I started getting calls from people in New York, Los Angeles, and Las Vegas, even before the draft, from people who wanted to represent me," he said. "In fact, one guy wanted to fly my wife and me out to Vegas just so I could talk to him. If I had gone I would have been ineligible for college ball; it would have made me a professional, so I couldn't do it. I also didn't feel I needed an agent at that stage. Several people told me to wait, if I get to the big leagues then I'll get one. To have one now would have been too much of a hassle."

After the draft and playing in A ball, Dave said it was too early to really think about the money.

"You don't think about big dollars because you're such a long way from them," Dave said. "You're just trying to get better and impress somebody. All you want to do is move up. Sometimes when you're home having a couple of beers you think about it. Heck, the major league minimum wage is going to be $40,000 a year and down here your first year you make $600 a month. So there's a big difference right away. But then you wake up and realize you've got to play again the next day. The dream is over for now."

Ed Amelung says his teammates talk about the money all the time. With first year players making $600 a month, he and his teammates often talk about how great things would be earning the big bread. Yet at the same time Ed doesn't think the era of the megabucks is all that good for baseball.

"I think it's getting a little out of hand," he said. "In some ways it's starting to hurt the game. Take a guy who signs a five-year contract. He may not work as hard the first couple of years, then he begins accelerating the pace as the end of the contract draws near. The players who put out all the time are the guys with real pride. My main motivation, however, is still a love for the game. The money is fine, but it's more important to me now to play."

Getting there and playing is obviously important. A guy can't make the money without doing that first. Both Del Crandall and Stan Wasiak feel the money in today's game has had its effect.

"There's more up ahead to go to," is the way Stan put it. "The money up there is definitely a goal for the young players. And how!"

Del Crandall agrees. "The money occupies a great deal of their time," he said. "But they're also aware that they can talk about it all they want, but until they produce on the field none of it will become a reality. I constantly try to impress this upon them. I also think all the kids today should eventually wind up with an agent. But the agent doesn't play and put the stats on the board. He can only help after you do that."

From his catbird nest above it all, Bill Schweppe has also seen the effect.

"I think because of the money situation today people are more inclined to question things, to demand things, and are more inclined to be their own persons than to submit to authority. You try to explain to them that playing in the minors is not a career per se. It's a schooling period, an apprenticeship, for which we pay you. No one pretends the minors are going to provide a player with a job like he would have working in industry or the private sector.

"I also think more players are going to have agents sooner because there are more agents around. Most of the major league players are tied up, so they're trying to get the guys at the minor league level. They catch him early and hopefully he'll make it to the majors and they'll have a client. It makes it a bit more difficult for us. Now, instead of dealing with one person, we've got to deal with two."

The money tree certainly doesn't grow as quickly in the minor leagues as it does in the Bigs, but its branches are reaching down and it does become a factor. But the prevalent opinion seems to be that you have to get there first, so there's no use in getting too excited about big money prospects before it can happen. But it certainly is a nice dream to have.

Playing in the minor leagues has also produced some other surprises for the players, and some things of interest that aren't heard about too often.

For instance, Ed Amelung as a first year player has already signed a glove and bat contract. He says most young players do this.

"You sign a five-year contract with the glove company and they supply you with the gloves," said Ed. "You get two in the spring and two before you go to winter ball. There's no way you're gonna need more than four in a year. Then, if you make it to the majors you're still wearing their glove. Kids will see it on television. Even now the local kids see the equipment you use and it sells the product. With a bat contract you get your autograph put on a bat. You also have the choice of $200 or a set of golf clubs. The glove contract doesn't pay anything except the glove. So neither is a big money deal."

For Dave Anderson there was still another surprise waiting his first year in pro ball.

"I didn't expect minor league fans to want autographs," he said. "But my first year at Vero I signed more things than I ever had in my life, and for everyone, little kids, old folks. I signed baseballs, programs, everything. I thought that wouldn't happen until I was higher up."

Dave Stewart will never forget a hotel in Boise, Idaho, where he stayed during his year in rookie ball.

"Everybody hated that place," he recalls. "It was the pits. There were old gas heaters with knobs on them that never worked, and the showers, if you could call them that, had three or four slow trickles of water. It was just a terrible place to stay."

An early taste of persistent sportswriters made Ricky Wright shake his head a few times last year.

"It was during the major league players' strike," he said. "Every time we turned around somebody was asking us about it. To be honest, it got to be old pretty fast. One night I was getting ready to pitch and about five guys came up to ask about the strike. I told them I was pretty much behind the players and sticking behind what they do. And they kept asking for more details, more details.

"Finally I said I've got to pitch tonight, what more can I say. But one guy wouldn't quit. He kept asking questions. Finally I said, hey, those guys (the striking players) are lucky. There's a lot of bass jumping out of those lakes and they can go ahead and catch them."

Jack Perconte probably won't forget a broken ankle he had in 1981 on a rather freak play. He was on third when the catcher let the pitch get away. So he broke for home.

"The pitcher came in to cover and decided he was gonna block the plate," he said. "But when I went into my slide, he tried to slide, too. I got there first and he drilled me with his spike right in the ankle. There was a spike wound and a break. It was really a dumb play and the thing I found disappointing was that he never told me he was sorry, even when I returned and faced him again. It would have been the gentlemanly thing to do."

One of Ted Power's biggest moments came when he met Dodger Hall of Famer Sandy Koufax, a larger-than-life legend, especially to young pitchers.

"The first time I met Sandy I was absolutely in awe," said Power. "All I wanted was his autograph. But after sitting and talking with him, I'm no longer awestruck by the man. Still, his record just blows me away. Later, I talked with him some more, played golf with him, and had a beer with him. I know that he's just like any other man, but it took awhile to realize that. He's just a heck of a nice guy who will go out of his way to help anyone."

When Don Crow went to spring training with the Dodgers for the first time in 1980 he wasn't sure how the veteran major leaguers would treat him. He found out what minor leaguers have learned for years. You meet all kinds.

"It was quite a thrill for me to be around all those guys I had been reading about for years and had watched on TV," Don said. "There were a surprising number of those who would watch you around the cage and give you a tip or two. And the pitchers in the bullpen respected my opinion when they asked about their stuff that day. That was a big deal for me and made me feel as if I was worth something.

"Some of the individual players were really nice to me. Dusty Baker comes to mind as one, and Burt Hooton was also super to me. Rick Monday was another player I really liked. But there were also a few guys who just won't give a minor leaguer the time of day. I guess that happens everywhere."

The eight players profiled in these pages had been in professional baseball from one to six years at the end of the 1981 season. Their experiences have naturally varied in some ways and have been similar in others. All of them have had their share of disappointments, ups and downs that have undoubtedly left a mark on their personalities. Yet the players on the whole say they don't want to change, don't want to be affected by the rigors of professional life and the delicate balance between success and failure. Nor do they want to be spoiled by the rewards, should they reach their goal in today's high priced market.

So they will continue to buck the odds, the odds that say just a small percentage ever make it from the minors to the Bigs. They follow the same road that thousands have traveled before and over which thousands will undoubtedly come in the years ahead. Perhaps now, however, the minor league experience can be summed up with two short anecdotes from a pair of first year players, Dave Anderson and Ed Amelung. These two tales seem to best serve as a microcosm of the highly emotional events that can occur when you're a professional ballplayer.

"The thing that hurt me the most since I've been in the minors happened in the clubhouse one day," Dave Anderson revealed. "We had just finished playing a game when one of my teammates walked in to take his uniform off and his locker was cleaned out. I couldn't believe it. I just sat and watched the guy.

"Then, in a few minutes, they called him into the office, gave him a pink slip, and said goodbye. He was being released. He just walked off the field and he was released. And I'm thinking, here's a guy who wanted to play professional baseball all his life, and he finally had a chance to make the dream come true. Then, bang, he's gone. Here's the check we owe you. Goodbye.

"I couldn't stop thinking about the disappointment on the guy's face and the thought that it could happen to me. I had never seen that done before. It was kind of an eerie feeling."

Ed Amelung, on the other hand, remembers his first time working out at Dodger Stadium with some of the major leaguers.

"Dusty Baker, the Dodgers leftfielder, was there every day," Ed recalled. "I couldn't believe how nice he was to everybody. He was just a great guy, would come out and shake my hand and say how you doin', Ed. Real down-to-earth. He made you feel that he was already a friend. He treated you like a human being. I know money and stardom can change people, but that's the way I'd like to be if I make it."

beetle bailey

CARTOON BOOKS
By Mort Walker

Enjoy more madcap adventures with Beetle, Sarge, Zero, Plato and all the gang at Camp Swampy!

☐	16894	**BEETLE BAILEY** $1.75
☐	16896	**BEETLE BAILEY: AT EASE** $1.75
☐	16895	**BEETLE BAILEY: FALL OUT LAUGHING** $1.75
☐	17266	**BEETLE BAILEY: GIVE US A SMILE** $1.50
☐	16897	**BEETLE BAILEY: I DON'T WANT TO BE HERE ANY MORE THAN YOU DO** $1.75
☐	17337	**BEETLE BAILEY: I THOUGHT YOU HAD THE COMPASS** $1.75
☐	16861	**BEETLE BAILEY: I'LL FLIP YOU FOR IT** $1.75
☐	12635	**BEETLE BAILEY: I'LL THROW THE BOOK AT YOU** $1.50
☐	16847	**BEETLE BAILEY: IS THAT ALL?** $1.75
☐	16899	**BEETLE BAILEY: ON PARADE** $1.75
☐	12659	**BEETLE BAILEY: SHAPE UP OR SHIP OUT** $1.50
☐	16898	**BEETLE BAILEY: WHAT IS IT NOW?** $1.75
☐	16977	**DON'T MAKE ME LAUGH, BEETLE BAILEY** $1.75
☐	17304	**PEACE, BEETLE BAILEY** $1.75
☐	17001	**TAKE A WALK, BEETLE BAILEY** $1.75
☐	17305	**TAKE TEN, BEETLE BAILEY** $1.75
☐	17332	**YOU'RE OUT OF HUP, BEETLE BAILEY** $1.75

Available wherever paperbacks are sold or use this coupon.

ACE TEMPO BOOKS
P.O. Box 400, Kirkwood, N.Y. 13795

Please send me the titles checked above. I enclose $_____.
Include $1.00 per copy for postage and handling. Send check or money order only. New York State residents please add sales tax.

NAME_____

ADDRESS_____

CITY_____ STATE_____ ZIP_____

T-03

Tempo Classics

☐ 17048	**ALICE IN WONDERLAND**	Lewis Carroll	$1.25
☐ 16968	**AESOP'S FABLES**		$1.95
☐ 15684	**BLACK BEAUTY**	Anna Sewell	$1.95
☐ 17338	**THE CALL OF THE WILD**	Jack London	$1.95
☐ 17323	**A CHRISTMAS CAROL**	Charles Dickens	$2.25
☐ 14596	**CAPTAINS COURAGEOUS**	Rudyard Kipling	$1.50
☐ 17015	**DR. JEKYLL AND MR. HYDE** Robert Louis Stevenson		$1.95
☐ 17104	**THE GLASS SLIPPER**	Eleanor Farjeon	$1.50
☐ 17339	**HEIDI**	Johanna Spyri	$1.95
☐ 17108	**HUCKLEBERRY FINN**	Samuel Clemens	$1.50
☐ 14151	**THE ILLUSTRATED NIGHT BEFORE CHRISTMAS** Alicia Austin		$1.95

Available wherever paperbacks are sold or use this coupon.

ACE TEMPO BOOKS
P.O. Box 400, Kirkwood, N.Y. 13795

Please send me the titles checked above. I enclose $_____.
Include $1.00 per copy for postage and handling. Send check or money order only. New York State residents please add sales tax.

NAME_____

ADDRESS_____

CITY_____STATE_____ZIP_____

T-02

Tempo Classics

☐ 17150	**JUNGLE BOOK** Rudyard Kipling $1.50	
☐ 16974	**KIDNAPPED** Robert Louis Stevenson $1.95	
☐ 17256	**LITTLE WOMEN** Louisa May Alcott $2.25	
☐ 16069	**PETER PAN** J.M. Barrie $1.25	
☐ 17238	**REBECCA OF SUNNYBOOK FARM** Kate Douglas Wiggin $1.75	
☐ 17148	**THE SWISS FAMILY ROBINSON** Johann Wyss $1.50	
☐ 17136	**TOM SAWYER** Samuel Clemens $1.50	
☐ 17121	**TREASURE ISLAND** Robert Lewis Stevenson $1.50	
☐ 17188	**THE WIND IN THE WILLOWS** Kenneth Grahame $1.50	
☐ 17134	**THE WIZARD OF OZ** L. Frank Baum $1.50	

Available wherever paperbacks are sold or use this coupon.

✦ ACE TEMPO BOOKS
P.O. Box 400, Kirkwood, N.Y. 13795

Please send me the titles checked above. I enclose $_____.
Include $1.00 per copy for postage and handling. Send check or money order only. New York State residents please add sales tax.

NAME_____

ADDRESS_____

CITY_____ STATE_____ ZIP_____

T-01